Successful
Business
Expansion

Successful Business Expansion

PRACTICAL STRATEGIES FOR PLANNING PROFITABLE GROWTH

Philip S. Orsino

John Wiley & Sons, Inc.
New York • Chichester • Brisbane • Toronto • Singapore

Copyright © 1994 by Philip S. Orsino
Published by John Wiley & Sons, Inc.

Library of Congress Cataloging-in-Publication Data:

Orsino, Philip S., 1954–
    Successful business expansion : Practical Strategies for Planning
    Profitable Growth / Philip S. Orsino
        p.   cm.
    Includes bibliographical references.
    ISBN 0-471-59737-6 (acid-free paper cloth)   ISBN 0-471-08624-X
    (acid-free paper paperback)
      1. Business—Management.   2. Industrial management.
    3. Business enterprises—Planning.   4. Success in business.
    I. Orsino, Philip S.   II. Title.
    HD69.S608   1994
    658.02′2—dc20   94-327

Printed in the United States of America
10 9 8 7 6 5 4 3 2 1

To my son, Joey

Acknowledgments

As I have tried to emphasize throughout this book, successful business expansion takes teamwork. So does successfully writing a book. Over the years, clients, colleagues, and friends have contributed much to the ideas collected here. While it is not possible to thank each one, I would like to recognize certain people without whom this project would not have materialized.

Betsy Matthews and Richard Birch collaborated with me on the organization and writing of the book and helped keep the project on track through their tenacity.

The input and support of Bob Tubbesing, Harley Ulster, and Charles Welker—Premdor's management team—have been, and continue to be, invaluable to me and to the success of the company. This book reflects their intelligence, experience, and enthusiasm.

Recognition is also due to Premdor's directors: Howard Beck, John Berton, John Cassaday, Peter Crossgrove, Richard Mauran, Alan McFarland, Joseph Rotman and Saul Spears; and to two past directors, Frank Hori and Peter Snucins. Their insight, critical advice, and wide-ranging knowledge of the business world have been essential to the company's global success. Without their support of our rapid growth, Premdor would not be the industry leader that it is today.

The energy and commitment of Premdor's managers and employees, who have experienced dramatic changes in operations and market conditions, are also to be saluted.

Finally, my family deserves special thanks for their understanding and acceptance of the many hours I have spent away from them, either in the process of guiding Premdor's growth or in the process of charting that growth in these pages.

Contents

Introduction   To Grow or Not to Grow—
                  The Question for the 1990s   1
Responding to the Changing Business Environment   1
Why Give Growth a Second Thought?   2
Control Is Key   3
Planning the Process, Knowing the Cost   4
What Will This Book Do for You?   5
How Did Premdor Do It?   5
Your Success   9

Part One   Planning for Success   **11**

1. Planning Your Expansion   13
      What Will Expansion Do for You?   13
      What Won't Expansion Do for You?   14
      Growth by What Route?   15
      Do You Have What It Takes?   16
      Assessing the Risk   31
      Putting the Plan on Paper   32
      Making the Commitment to Change   32

2. Planning Your Financing   35
      Financing Fundamentals   35
      Your Planning Is Only as Good as Your Information   36
      Developing Your Business Plan   37
      What Does It Cost to Expand?   46

Where Will You Get Your Financing?   50
Expansion at What Price?   58

Part Two   Expanding at Home   **61**

3. Expanding Internally: Getting More from Your
    Current Markets   63
    The Best Defense Includes a Good Offense   63
    Are You Ready to Expand Internally?   64
    Know Your Customers' Needs   67
    Improve Your Marketing to Improve Your Market Share   71
    Expansion Through Innovation   75
    The More You Know, the More You Get   77

4. Going on the Offensive   79
    Expanding into New Domestic Markets   79
    There's No Place Like Home (and Home Is Not Like
      Any Place Else)   80
    Expanding Through Franchising   86
    Expanding Through Alliances   91
    Don't Just Make Your Piece of the Pie Bigger—
      Make the Pie Bigger   98

5. Expanding Through Acquisitions and Mergers   101
    Advice on Acquisitions and Mergers from the
      Horse's Mouth   101
    The Benefits of Tying the Corporate Knot   101
    Your Future May Depend on It   103
    What Can Go Wrong?   104
    Planning the Process   105
    Courtship   107
    Engagement   108
    Tying the Knot   121
    Working to Make the Marriage Last   122
    Monitoring the Corporate Marriage   126

Part Three   Expanding Abroad   **129**

6. Analyze Your Position and Assess Your Export Potential   131
    Can You Afford Not to Export?   131
    What Exporting Can Do for You   133

What Exporting Can't Do for You   134
What Opportunities Exist?   135
The Challenge of Commitment   136
Planning the Exporting Process   136
Look in the Mirror   137
Learn from Foreign Competitors   143
Prepare to Manage Change   145
Prepare to Foster Commitment   148

7. Researching Potential Export Markets   153
    Targeting Markets   154
    Developing a Short List of Target Markets   156
    Gathering Information   167
    Evaluating the Risks and Rewards of Markets on Your
        Short List   170

8. Developing and Implementing Your Export Plan   171
    Lay the Groundwork in Writing   171
    Key Questions Your Plan Should Address   172
    How Will You Track Your Progress?   180
    Implementing Your Plan   188

Part Four   Expanding for Your Own Good   **191**

9. Expansion as a Process of Continuous Improvement   193
    Evaluate Your Product or Service Through Your
        Customers' Eyes   194
    Review Production Processes   195
    Consider New Distribution Methods   196
    Research New Approaches to Marketing   196
    Look for New Product or Market Opportunities   197
    Reassess Your Financial Base   198
    Upgrade Your Accounting Systems   199
    Be Aware of Currency Fluctuations   200
    Gain Employees' Commitment to Your Expansion Plan   200
    Evaluate Your Management Team and Structure   201
    Expand Your Knowledge Base   202

Understand Your Role as CEO   203
Manage the Risk Involved in Expanding   204

Appendix A. Premdor's Environmental Due Diligence
             Checklist   207

Appendix B. Summary of Premdor's Due Diligence
             Checklist   213

Index   229

INTRODUCTION

To Grow or Not to Grow—
The Question for the 1990s

Responding to the Changing
Business Environment

The reason for reading and writing this book can be summed up in one word: change. The post-World War II business environment was defined by small regional markets, protective tariffs, and foreign competition that, for the most part, was not as industrially advanced as North American manufacturers. Some thought that would be a world without end. Then the effects of technological advances, increased competition from the Far East and Europe, free trade agreements, and the recession all seemed to collide in the late 1980s, bringing radical change to business.

The new environment in which North American businesses must now operate is affected not only by what happens in our state, province, country, and continent, but by what happens around the world. Our competitors are no longer just the business across the street, across the country, or even across the border, but companies across the ocean and across the globe.

The impact of these fundamental changes has created its share of uncertainty, anxiety, and stress. In response, business has two options. One is to sit tight, hope things work out (that is, go back to the way they were), and risk losing everything. The other is to catch the global wave and grow.

Yet, growth is suffering a bad reputation today. Management gurus and business pundits tell us that the 1990s is the decade of small is beautiful and big is bad. Across North America, companies are busy downsizing or even actively avoiding growth. Growth is seen as an embarrassing episode of 1980s excess, a binge from which we've sobered up. In the aftermath, we look back and see a dramatic string of wrecked companies, large and small, littering the corporate landscape. Most of those wrecks are companies that grew in the 1980s. And the prevailing logic is that they failed because they grew.

Don't believe it. Companies don't fail because they grow. They fail because they don't *plan* their growth. They don't know why they are growing, they don't know how to grow, and they mistakenly believe that growth will solve their problems.

In fact, it is more likely that a North American company will fail because it *doesn't* grow than because it does grow. Whether growth is achieved through expanding product lines, building new plants, expanding domestic markets, exporting, acquiring another business, or forming strategic alliances, many would argue that now more than ever growth is one of the keys to corporate health and profitability. In tough, competitive times, it's a fallacy for most companies to believe that they can afford to stand still.

Yet, any business in the 1990s that has second thoughts about expansion is on the right track—because thinking about growth, and planning it properly, are the keys to growing successfully.

Why Give Growth a Second Thought?

Here are nine good reasons to reconsider the benefits of expansion:

1. Expansion boosts profitability.

2. It also helps to reduce risk. Geographical expansion—moving into new markets across the country, the continent, or the world—is an effective way to diversify and distribute your corporate eggs among more than one basket. Expanding the range of products or services you offer has the same protective effect.

3. Expansion helps you learn about and understand your industry, both at home and abroad, and thus helps you stay competitive.

4. Expansion allows you to ensure a source of supply and take greater advantage of distribution channels.

5. Expansion helps to ensure your survival. If you are in just one market, you are more vulnerable than a competitor who is in twenty markets.

6. Growing makes your company better. The more markets you deal in, the more you are forced to take a long, hard look at your products since customers in new markets are often more demanding than your current customers. The more demanding your customers are, the more your product quality improves. When you sell in foreign markets or in domestic markets on the other side of the country, you can't afford to be sloppy—problems are too costly to fix long distance. So, dealing in different markets actually helps you deal in your home market.

7. Growing helps you cut costs. Dealing in new markets often alerts you to opportunities to source raw materials at a better price. Becoming a low-cost producer helps you compete better not only in foreign markets but also at home.

8. Expansion makes you more efficient. It gives you the opportunity to see different and often better systems at work elsewhere and put them to work for you. Companies often have certain systems in place because they are easy, not because they are better. Expansion exposes you to better ways of doing things.

9. Expansion keeps your company from being left behind. The more markets you deal in, the more you see and the more you learn about your product line and your industry. Exposure to innovative ideas gives you an edge over competitors who've decided not to venture further afield. And being tuned in also makes your customers more interested in you. Think of it as being at a dinner party. Would you rather sit next to someone who is well-traveled and aware of what's going on in numerous places or someone who never goes more than a few miles from home?

Control Is Key

Given all the benefits of expansion, what went wrong in the expansion-crazy eighties and why is business so averse to expansion today?

In the eighties, growth was typically high speed and flat out. But it wasn't thought out. It was growth for growth's sake. It wasn't planned. It wasn't controlled. And that is why it so often failed.

Entrepreneurs of the eighties treated expansion like a game of blackjack. They won once or twice and then kept on playing until they lost. They made deals, their share prices went up, they could raise more money, they continued to make deals. People didn't bat an eye if they heard about a financial holding company that leveraged out an aerospace company that two weeks earlier leveraged out a building products company that in the previous year was part of a chemical company. In the end, of course, the healthy, profitable companies were destroyed to support new ventures, and ultimately the new ventures failed, too.

If there is a lesson for the nineties in the wreckage of the eighties, it's that sound business planning never goes out of style. Those who don't know why they are growing or haven't analyzed how growth fits in with their long-term goals spin out of control.

Planning the Process, Knowing the Cost

If successful growth depends on planning, successful planning depends on careful self-assessment, a process that was all too often overlooked in the 1980s.

Many companies that grow and go under fail to ask themselves, and take the time to answer, the fundamental question: How will expansion affect our existing business? How will it affect our customers, suppliers, managers, and employees? Will growth destroy what we've already built, or will it strengthen our position? One of the problems of eighties-style growth was that it was all too often growth at any price. In the nineties, the smart question is: growth at what price?

Make no mistake about it—expansion changes your company. If you are not well-organized now, growing will cripple you. If you can't walk, how will you run? Growth makes everything bigger. If you've got problems and you grow, you'll end up with bigger problems. In the eighties, when money was loose and growth was easy, many businesses thought that growth would solve their problems, or at least make them go away. As we have seen, they were mistaken.

Another classic mistake of eighties-style growth was that companies were in a hurry. So many opportunities, so much available financing. But, once again, so little planning. Successful growth occurs one bite at a time, with control. A business that is growing successfully and according to plan never takes another bite until it has swallowed the last one. Then it digests before growing again.

In the nineties, the go-slower attitude is the right attitude toward growth. Why? Expansion not only demands a firm commitment of time, money, and effort, its effects reverberate throughout a company also. If you are not on firm ground with your finances, management, employees, customers, and suppliers, you won't be able to withstand the tremors.

What Will This Book Do for You?

In this book, you will learn how to decide whether growth is for you, and you will learn how to plan your expansion process, should you decide to go ahead. As a practical resource book and planning guide, it will help you answer questions about what is the best way for you to grow, why and when you should make your moves, and how you should make them.

Chapter 1 explains what expansion can—and cannot—do for you, what commitments it entails, and how expansion will affect your company. In this chapter, you will learn how to assess whether you are ready to expand. Chapter 2 explains what it takes to finance growth and will help you analyze whether your company is financially prepared to expand. You will learn about what goes into good financial planning, why it is the key to successful growth, and what types of financing you are likely to find in the tight money 1990s.

Chapters 3 through 8 tell you how to expand in your current domestic markets, in new domestic markets, and in foreign markets. These chapters describe the procedures for identifying, researching, and targeting markets; analyzing risks; and mapping out an expansion plan. Chapter 9 is designed to help you with the process of managing the changes that expansion will bring to your company.

Because each chapter deals with the process of planning for healthy growth, the information will not go out of date.

How Did Premdor Do It?

Indeed, the management team at Premdor today has been practicing what we preach in this book for over a decade. During that time, we have grown from being a small, Canadian start-up business to being one of the world's largest manufacturer and distributor of wood doors for new residential construction, home repair and renovation, and commercial use. While our single plant used to turn out 1,500 doors per day a decade ago, we now build over 55,000 doors per day (14 million per year) in 18 locations in three countries. Here is what happened.

In 1983, I left my position as a partner at a public accounting firm to become president and CEO of Century Wood Door Limited. Century was a new, one-plant operation in suburban Toronto that manufactured interior flush doors, the kind used for closets, bedrooms, bathrooms, and hallways, and that are made by sandwiching a wood frame and a hollow or solid core between two door faces of plywood or hardboard. With growth as one of our key corporate objectives, Century acquired a louvre door (these doors look like shutters) plant in Quebec, started a solid wood door (with vertical and horizontal components, like French doors and most wood exterior doors) plant in 1985, and established a flush door plant in Montreal in 1986. In 1987, we acquired a manufacturer of doors and prefinished door mouldings based near Vancouver, British Columbia. By this time, the company was producing about 8,000 doors a day.

By 1988, we anticipated that a major portion of our future growth would be in the United States. Because we wanted to create a significant presence in the United States and we wanted to do it quickly, we decided that, rather than build from scratch or export from Canada, we would acquire an established U.S. door manufacturer. Through its operations in Florida, Texas, Alabama, and Virginia, the company we purchased in 1988 offered us capacity, distribution, an experienced management team, and sales in excess of $50 million. In 1988, we also established a sales office in the United Kingdom.

By 1989, continuing changes in the marketplace meant that the door industry in both Canada and the United States faced a number of challenges and, for those who were prepared, opportunities. Specifically, the implementation of the Canada–U.S. Free Trade Agreement meant that customs duties on wood doors of North American origin traded between Canada and the United States were phased out over a five-year period beginning in January 1989. In addition, as world trade barriers began to relax, the market for wood doors was becoming more globalized. At the same time, North American housing construction starts were beginning to contract sharply, and the recession was just around the corner.

In order to be in a position to capitalize on the globalization of trade and continue to grow despite the slowing economy, Century orchestrated a merger with its largest Canadian competitor, Premdor, in 1989. In its first six years, Century had grown into a $140 million a year business. At the time of the merger, Premdor, which began manufacturing doors in 1961, was slightly larger in sales and had been listed on the Toronto and Montreal stock exchanges since 1986. The combined entity, of which I became president and CEO, retained the Premdor name. This company was better than either of the two individual companies had been—and that gave us advantages. We could become more competitive in the North American door industry. We could also achieve more specialization of plants in strategic locations. This increased our production flexibility, enabling us to react more effectively to changing circumstances.

Because of the merger, we also were able to rationalize and restructure several of our respective operations. This allowed the new Premdor to reduce operating costs through reducing inventory levels; eliminating duplicate marketing and sales programs; closing certain plant and production facilities; and eliminating duplicate selling, warehousing, and administrative expenses. In addition, reorganizing distribution facilities allowed us to diversify product lines and improve customer service. We also now had the resource of a management team that combined depth of experience with entrepreneurial and financial skill. Thus, the merger enabled Premdor to become a more aggressive global competitor through:

♦ Efficiency gains.

♦ Expansion of U.S. operations.

♦ An increase in exports to offshore countries.

♦ Improvement of service and distribution to customers.

♦ The development of new product lines.

Since 1989, we have continued to make acquisitions when they meet our strategic objectives. For example, a significant U.S. acquisition, completed in 1991, provided us with a more diversified product line and enabled Premdor to approximately double its sales of interior residential doors in the United States. The purchase also enabled us to cover the midwest and central United States more effectively. In 1992, we purchased a California-based door company with annual sales of approximately $15 million, thus strengthening our presence in the western United States. In the same year, we also acquired the assets of two other companies, one Canadian and one U.S., giving us access to machinery and inventory at favorable prices. In 1993, Premdor made its first foreign acquisition--the purchase of a French door manufacturer with annual sales of approximately $15 million. This state-of-the-art facility will allow Premdor to produce in France a line of doors that we currently export to Europe. In early 1994, we acquired a second door company in France, thus continuing our geographic expansion in Western Europe.

Today, approximately 70 percent of Premdor's business is conducted in the United States, 25 percent is conducted in Canada, and 5 percent is carried out in Europe. We produce over 800 standard types and sizes of doors and claim 30 percent of the North American door market. Our worldwide sales exceed $500 million. Over $10 million of those sales are derived from exports, primarily to the United Kingdom and Europe, but also to Mexico, the Middle East, and Asia. The company's sales of doors have grown at an average annual compound growth rate of 30 percent since 1988.

Since 1990, Premdor has raised $135 million in four equity issues. At December 31, 1990, share prices for Premdor on the Toronto Stock Exchange were $1.70, with 13,621,772 shares outstanding; by December 31, 1993, share prices climbed to $15-1/8, with 35,873,992 shares outstanding. In April 1993, Premdor was listed on the New York Stock Exchange— only the twenty-ninth company in Canadian history to do so.

In certain ways, Premdor has been a contrarian company. The 1989 merger with Century marked the beginning of a phase of significant growth for us. Yet that was exactly when the wheels were beginning to fall off the growth train of many other companies. The bulk of our expansion has occurred in the worst of economic times—the recession of the early 1990s. And our corporate philosophy—to be highly focused on expanding markets for one product line so that we don't dilute our strength, which is manufacturing and distributing doors—runs counter to the prevailing wisdom of diversification that characterized business throughout the 1980s. As well, in an era of high tech, we sell one of the oldest, simplest, and most low-tech products imaginable—doors. Yet, we've grown from being a Canadian company to being a North American company to being a global competitor. And we have done it on our own terms and according to our own timing.

While Premdor's strategy of pursuing internal growth, acquisitions, a merger, and exporting may not have exposed us to *all* the complexities of expansion, it probably has exposed us to most of them. For that reason, we believe that our experience can serve as a useful guideline and help shorten the expansion learning curve for others.

Your Success

Going ahead with expansion is serious business—you can stop but you can't go back. Your business cannot grow without experiencing changes. But if you've planned your process, your company will grow strong and you will avoid the growing, growing, gone syndrome that plagued so many companies in the eighties. Opportunities for healthy growth, for growth that fits your company's particular strengths, exist in the 1990s. Should you ignore them because of the legacy of growth gone wrong in the eighties? Or should you learn to grow the right way in the nineties?

PART ONE
Planning for Success

CHAPTER 1

Planning Your Expansion

This chapter focuses on the following issues:

♦ What expansion can, and cannot, do for you.

♦ What commitments expansion demands.

♦ How growth can affect your existing business.

♦ How to assess whether your company is ready to grow.

♦ How to begin planning your expansion.

What Will Expansion Do for You?

In the long run, the most important thing that expansion will do for your company is to make it more profitable.

But expansion will pay off in other ways, too, both in the short run and the long run. The steps a company can take to expand may not immediately boost the bottom line, but they may, for example, benefit the company by:

♦ Reducing vulnerability to seasonal or economic cycles.

♦ Protecting existing market share.

♦ Keeping competitors from gaining market share.

♦ Ensuring continued access to raw materials.

♦ Helping it take greater advantage of distribution channels.

====

A t Premdor, our business is making and distributing wood doors and mouldings for new residential construction, home repair and renovation, and commercial use. It's both a seasonal and a cyclical business, tied to the always volatile construction industry. For us, reducing the impact of stop-and-start seasonal demand and roller-coaster economic cycles is a key to increased profitability.

Many in business think that the way to reduce the impact of seasonal variations in sales is to diversify product lines. But the problem with that strategy is that the more products you add, the more difficult the company can become to manage. That was one of the problems with the 1980s style of growth. Companies that diversified lost control. Most are now breaking apart, selling off acquisitions, and getting back to the basics.

At Premdor, we tried something different to reduce our vulnerability to cycles—we stuck to the same product lines but diversified our markets. Now, for example, when demand for building products is down in one part of the country, the company can still do well because we also operate in other parts of North America and in Europe where markets might be more buoyant. We are no longer affected by what happens in a single market.

If the bottom line is that you expand to make more money, sometimes that means not incurring losses when the cycle is down.

====

What Won't Expansion Do for You?

If you are contemplating growth as a way to solve problems, don't, because it won't. In fact, growth initially may cause some problems for your company. It always introduces complications and change, which many see as problems.

And expansion will not instantly result in a rosy bottom line. Every form of growth requires a significant investment. It literally could be years before you see a positive return on that investment. If you acquire a company or merge, the new operation might need some degree of rationalization, which could, depending on the situation, result in short-term costs and require further investment. However, once these costs have been incurred, profits should improve significantly. If you develop a new market, entry costs could offset profits in that market, perhaps for several years. If you introduce a new product, you may be looking at a two- to three-year period, or longer, before all your development and start-up costs are written off and you begin to see your new line producing a profit.

Finally, you should be aware that growth most often leads to more growth, which, in turn, leads to more growth. Even though you consolidate and digest between growth spurts, profits may not be optimized until you have achieved the level of expansion that is dictated by the growth strategy you have chosen.

Growth by What Route?

Your basic business strategy will help you determine which type of expansion is best for your company. For example:

♦ If your current success formula is based on selling your product or service at a lower price than your competitors, you may want to pursue growth that will enable you to source materials more cheaply than competitors so that you maintain your price advantage.

♦ If you offer better service and quality than competitors, you may want to grow in ways that allow you to improve production and delivery capabilities.

♦ If you want to be less vulnerable to seasonal cycles, then you might consider growth through expanding your markets as Premdor has done.

♦ If you want to be more flexible or adaptable to changing economic cycles, you might grow through a merger or an acquisition. Larger companies have more alternatives in tough times. And in this sense, expansion is a survival strategy.

If you are a one-plant operation and you have to close down, you will be out of business. If you have more than one plant, you have more than one option. At the same time, you have more ways of benefiting from good times. Currently, Premdor builds about 55,000 doors a day but has the capacity to build more. When the economy is good and demand for building products is strong, that capacity gives us a lot more potential than a company with a capacity to build only 5,000 doors a day.

Bear in mind, too, that as conditions in your industry, in the economy, and in world trade change, your current formula for success may not work in five years. If you don't grow, finding the perfect niche as a small player also might be a viable survival strategy. Staying still, though, probably guarantees failure. If everything around you is changing, you had better change, too—or be left behind.

Do You Have What It Takes?

While considering which path to growth is best for your company, you also must determine whether you've got what it takes to grow without going under. And that means taking a long, hard look in the mirror.

Across all industries, certain characteristics are common to companies that expand successfully. Does your company fit the profile presented in Figure 1-1?

If your company doesn't score on all ten points, you probably need to lay more groundwork before expanding.

If you think your firm fits the profile of a company that is likely to expand successfully, take a closer look—this time at your resources. Bear in mind that every company has limited resources, including time and people's ability. Do you really have the resources you need to expand?

The Eight Essentials—Your Core Resources

The list of eight of the core resources that every business needs in order to expand successfully follows your company's profile (Figure 1-1).

Figure 1-1. **Profile of a company that is likely to expand successfully. It . . .**

---

1. Thinks like a bigger company.
2. Sees markets next door, across the border, and even around the world as its potential markets.
3. Has proven ability in strategic planning.
4. Prepares written business plans and has the discipline to follow them; does not have a "last minute" or "crisis" management mentality.
5. Regularly undertakes careful self-assessment; knows its strengths and weaknesses and compensates where necessary.
6. Is meeting demand for its product or services in current markets.
7. Has sound resources in the areas of production, materials, people, finance, time, and patience.
8. Sees change as a challenge, not a problem to be avoided.
9. Looks at growth as a way to strengthen the business, not as a way to solve problems.
10. Has asked itself how expansion will affect the existing business.

---

1. Commitment.

2. Knowledge.

3. Adaptability.

4. Financial strength.

5. People.

6. Communication.

7. Capacity.

8. Time and patience.

You need to assess how rich your company is in each resource before you can decide whether to go ahead with expansion. You also will need to come back to this list to test your company's state of readiness each time you decide to take another growth step. For example, if you currently are thinking of entering new markets at home, review the list to determine whether your company is up to the challenge and has adequate resources to support such growth. If, at a later date, you think you want to expand further by exporting, come back to the list and reassess your state of readiness. No matter what type of growth you are contemplating, or when you are contemplating it, the core list should be your first stop.

Reviewing the list not only will help you begin to plan your growth, it also will help keep you on track in managing what you've already got.

1. Commitment.   In thinking about the process you must go through if you are to expand successfully, fostering commitment within your organization is key. Can you do it?

Successful growth isn't haphazard. It isn't the result of an opportunity that happens to fall into your lap. Successful growth is planned. It is the result of a decision to pursue growth as one of the major objectives of your corporate strategy. Once you've decided to grow—through increasing capacity, adding a new product line, forming a strategic alliance, acquiring another company, or by another means—there is no second-guessing it.

A t Premdor, expanding the company is as much a part of what we do as making and distributing doors. These days, our industry is experiencing widespread rationalization as the market changes from a regional to a North American one. Eventually, there will be niche players and substantial players in the door industry, and our goal is to be one of the latter.

Once you are committed to making growth one of your strategic objectives, pursuing it is no different from pursuing any other corporate objective, such as purchasing a new piece of equipment, upgrading computer systems, or motivating your sales force.

However, if even one person at a relatively senior level in your organization isn't convinced that the company should grow, you will run up against problems. As president, it is your job to explain to your management team, and to other employees, how growth will benefit the company. (Try reviewing the Introduction's list of nine good reasons to grow.) If they don't buy into it, it is because either:

♦ They won't buy into it no matter how good your reasons are, in which case there's no place for them on the team; or

♦ Your reasons are not very good.

As you think about whether you want to commit your company to growth, check your motives:

♦ Is ego driving your desire to grow?

♦ Are you growing to gain increased personal power and prestige?

♦ Is your plan based solely on the fact that you are already successful?

If you admit to any of these motives, watch out—you probably are experiencing the "Midas Touch" syndrome. And your business may suffer as a consequence.

Classic examples of growth gone wrong in the 1980s and early 1990s are also classic examples of the "Midas Touch" syndrome. Think of real estate developers who seemingly believed that there was a never-ending supply of corporate tenants and thus built megaproject after megaproject until the bottom fell out of the commercial building market. Think of companies that bought retail operation after retail operation, using the resources and leverage gained from one purchase to prop up the next until, like a house of cards, the empire collapsed. Or think of the once high profile high fliers who thought nothing of having a finger in industries as diverse as real estate, transportation, and manufacturing because they apparently believed that every business deal they touched would turn to gold. If nothing else, such examples should serve as cautionary tales, and this chapter should force you to honestly assess your reasons for considering expansion.

Your current success may be a requirement for growth, but it's not a reason for growth. And going bankrupt is neither prestigious nor an effective way to gain power. In business, as in gambling, the odds in the long run are against those with the "Midas Touch" syndrome.

In businesses that are partnerships, it's not uncommon for one party to want to go ahead with expansion while the other balks. Sometimes one partner doesn't want to take the risk, while the other partner is eager to move ahead. Such differences are often resolved when one partner buys out the other. In this type of situation, and in situations where directors or shareholders might be reluctant to make a commitment to growth, a motive check is also in order. Ultimately, long-term profitability and long-term corporate success are the only sound motives for growth.

2. Knowledge.   Knowledge is power. And knowledge of your industry and the economy is key to expanding successfully.

I n the past three years, Premdor has made a number of acquisitions, some within months of each other. One reason we have been able to make those moves is our accumulated knowledge of the door industry. We've made it a point to know who our competitors are, who is doing well, and who isn't. Keeping that knowledge up-to-date has been a critical part of our growth strategy and thus has allowed us to negotiate deals at the right time and at the right price.

One of the important benefits of developing a highly focused picture of your industry and the economic conditions affecting it is that, in the process, you also develop a sense of timing. This sense of timing is one of your best assets—it means that your expansion is not left to chance and that you know what moves to make and when to make them.

Often, the timing for taking certain growth steps is the reverse of what people think. A recession, for example, presents some great opportunities for growth, especially through mergers and acquisitions. Management at a target company is likely to be more open to the idea of sitting down at the negotiating table, and prices will be lower than in good times. Recessions also present opportunities to build market share. If you have a new idea that distinguishes you from your competitors, clients who are trying to boost their own sales are more apt to listen. Tough times can also be good times to form strategic alliances because, in tough times, people are all ears.

Your skill at spotting good opportunities in bad times is directly related to the breadth, depth, and quality of your knowledge about your industry.

M uch of Premdor's growth has taken place during the worst of economic times—1989 to 1993. Our approach to selling doors is heavily weighted toward innovative marketing and merchandising. When times are good and the building supply outlets that are our market think they are selling all they can, they are not as interested in hearing about new approaches. But, in tough times, customers and potential customers stop and listen when they hear that we are going to offer them point-of-sale displays, training clinics for their staff, and in-store decorating seminars for their customers. They are anxious to find new ways to increase their sales.

Your ability to identify good opportunities in good times is also a product of knowledge. In good times, growth strategies change. For example, when the economy is strong, it's tough to make acquisitions. People don't want to sell because they are doing well, and, even if you can convince them, they probably want too much money. Opportunities for mergers and strategic alliances don't arise nearly as often in good economic times either.

However, if times are good, your company is probably doing well, too. That means you have more money to invest in exports, in new product development, in new ways of merchandising, and in trying to enter new markets. And establishing your position in a new market will happen much faster in good times than in bad.

Your knowledge base can also give you an edge in another way. Today, many industries, especially in the manufacturing sector, are aging. Like the door industry, they started up in the 1950s and most, if not all, of their management worked its way up through the ranks from the plant floor. Current management in these aging industries is often no exception. Its experience is in production, not in professional finance, marketing, or merchandising. Thus, if yours is an aging industry but you have put together a management team with depth of experience in finance, marketing, and merchandising, you have an advantage over competitors who are strictly production oriented. Your financial know-how can help you build a solid base on which to grow larger than your competitors, and your marketing expertise can help you increase market share at their expense.

3. Adaptability.   A successful company that expands may find that its formula for success breaks down on a larger scale or doesn't work in another market.

How adaptable is your business? To a degree, your answer will depend on whether you sell products or services. If you run a hands-on, personal services business in Toronto, for instance, it probably will be difficult to open up shop 200 miles away in Detroit, much less 3,000 miles away in Vancouver or Los Angeles. If you make snow shovels, chances are you won't expand into the southern United States. When you consider whether growth is for you, you have to look at what you offer, the conditions for which your product or service is meant, and the specifications. Some businesses just are not as adaptable as others.

In Premdor's case, our desire to expand throughout North America and beyond makes sense because doors are used around the world—they are truly a global product.

To a certain extent, the geographic location of your business also affects your adaptability. If you want to export, are you in a good location to do so? If your business is in Nevada and you want to export to Europe, are you in the right place? Perhaps it would be better to set your sights on the Far East, provided that your product or service is adaptable to that market.

4. Financing.   Financing is a resource. If it's scarce, it's like running out of inventory. No matter how many orders you have, you won't be able to fill them unless you have sufficient financial resources.

Chapter 2 explains in detail the type of financial resources and planning needed to grow without going under. In brief, your financial resources must include good financial reporting systems, a healthy balance sheet, and a lack of debt or low debt to equity ratio.

5. Communication.   Whenever a company initiates change, people feel uncertain. When your company takes a growth step, uncertainty about its new direction will not be limited to those within the organization. It will also be felt by those outside the company—customers and suppliers. Thus, an important part of planning your expansion process is determining how you can reassure employees and clients about the changes taking place. The best way to reassure people is through communication, and lots of it. Keeping people informed, as much as possible, helps them to feel that they are part of the process.

The responsibility for communication falls squarely on the shoulders of the CEO. He or she must be sensitive to the fears and doubts that come with change. This is especially important if the organization is growing through a merger or an acquisition. In such cases, employees are likely to feel threatened by potential job loss, the addition of new management, and, in the case of a merger, questions about which company "won," which "lost," and how a change in the balance of power will affect them.

As mentioned earlier, commitment to growth has to come from the top. If you are convinced that growth will benefit your company, even if there are certain costs, such as job loss, it's up to you to convince your employees that, in the long run, growth is in everyone's best interest. It's up to you to motivate them to work with change and to feel positive about the fact that the company is working hard to be competitive. Everyone must buy in and communication must be open and frequent so that employees do not feel threatened.

Do you, as CEO, have the time, sensitivity, skills, and resources to handle the communication that growth demands? Is there a member of your management team who could take on these responsibilities? Or should you think about hiring a professional consultant to help you:

♦ Plan internal communications.

♦ Identify and deal with issues that might worry personnel, including structural changes within the company or layoffs.

◆ Determine how to deal with rumors.

◆ Work with and reassure employees whose job responsibilities might change radically.

When Premdor acquired three competitors in 1991, people within the company worried about the changes that might occur. Who would run the operations? Would new managers come on the scene? Would jobs be lost? Would people be transferred? There was a lot of hand-holding done within the company, not only at the time of the acquisitions but also on an ongoing basis. And, that hand-holding was based on communication.

There were numerous meetings to bring together key managers, some of whom had never met before. And there were numerous meetings to bring together managers and employee groups. During that intensive two-month period, our major goal was to get everyone on the bandwagon by explaining where the company was headed, why, and how each person fit into the picture.

Three years later, we're still committed to making communication a priority. We publish a quarterly newsletter for our staff that deals specifically with the company's growth so that everyone, from managers to machinists, is psychologically involved in the continuing expansion process. The result of keeping our people informed is that they are proud of the company and excited about the future—not a bad return on our investment in communication.

As noted, you also have to be aware of how your expansion will affect your existing customers and suppliers and their perceptions of your company. If you are growing in order to provide better service or to enhance your marketing capabilities, make sure to let your clients know specifically how the changes in your company will benefit them. If you are growing through a merger or an acquisition, your clients may worry that the known entity they are used to dealing with will no longer provide what they need. Why not consider making a corporate video that explains your new direction and inviting your clients to see it? By making the effort to keep them informed, you are letting them know that they are important to your company's future success.

———

A few years ago, after Premdor had grown to double its pre-merger size, one of our divisions switched over to a computerized ordering and distribution system to simplify, speed up, and improve service to our customers. However, as is the case with introducing any new computerized system, both our staff and our customers had to go through a learning curve before the system really began to benefit them. Staff had to get up to speed on the computer programs, on procedures, and on training. Part of providing improved service meant that orders had to be placed by certain deadlines for guaranteed delivery. Thus, customers who formerly would telephone us half a dozen times a day to place or change orders had to adapt.

A short time after we implemented the new system, one of our customers commented to a sales manager that while growth might be good for Premdor, it wasn't good for him. When the sales manager probed a little more deeply, he found that the client was having some problems getting used to the new ordering system and that he linked these problems (encouraged perhaps by one of our competitors) to our ongoing expansion.

As you grow, it's important to be aware that your customers' perceptions of your company may change. Keep your ears to the ground and be prepared to take the time to reassure clients that changes in your business will benefit them. We explain to our Canadian customers that a key advantage of dealing with us is our involvement in other markets—we bring a lot of resources to the table. It's not only the actual impact that growth may have on your existing customers that you have to watch, it's also the perceived impact.

---

6. People.   Your people are every bit as important as your planning and your product or service when you expand. If you don't have the right management, the right number of people, and people with the right abilities and capabilities, you risk not only that your expansion won't work, but also that it will weaken your existing business. One of your ongoing jobs is to ensure that you have the ability to attract, and keep, the best people you can find. You not only want to build a winning team—you also want to build such a reputation for winning that all others in the industry want to be on your team.

While human resources issues are covered in more detail in later chapters in the book, you should stop now to consider the following basic questions:

♦ If you set up shop in a new market, who will run the show? Are you willing to hire new management, or will you transfer someone from your current operation to head up the new one? If you do transfer that person, who will take on his or her previous responsibilities?

O ne of our competitors in Toronto had a sales manager who was so good, the company transferred him to run its new plant in Atlanta, Georgia—and it was a disaster. He was in a job and a marketplace in which he was lost. Not only did the company suffer from not having one of its best managers in Toronto, it also failed to make a good showing in its new target market. With one ill-planned move, the company lost twice.

♦ If you plan to increase sales, will you have to increase staff? In which areas—sales, accounting, manufacturing, management? Or can you, or outside experts, develop systems to accommodate the changes growth will bring?

O ver the last four years as Premdor has grown, we've
brought onboard additional senior financial people, a vice
president of sales and marketing, and, most recently, a vice president who was formerly a partner at a law firm. This last addition
is part and parcel of being a public company, dealing with reams
of regulations, and acquiring a number of companies in a relatively short time. Expanding creates entirely new areas of
responsibility. Administration becomes more complex. Doubling in size could mean significantly expanding your administrative team. So keeping an eye on management is essential to
maintaining control while you grow.

◆ If you merge, will you have too many people on staff? Can someone in-house deal with counseling those who lose their jobs, or should you
bring in outside help during the transition?

◆ If you plan to expand through acquisition, in theory, you'll acquire
instant management. But what if key managers from the acquired company
quit the day after you close the deal?

A company that Premdor acquired several years ago got into
trouble with an earlier acquisition of its own. The day that
company completed its transaction, half the management at the
target company quit, including the key salespeople who went to
work for the competition. The senior team at the company making the acquisition just assumed that everyone at the target company would stay and never paid any attention to that part of the
transaction. The people who left, however, felt that they had
built the company and saw no reason to stay on when, in their
opinion, the owner had just walked away with full pockets.

    If the people in a company are essential to its continued
success, and they often are, the prospective new owner should

consider signing them to employment contracts, consider getting noncompeting agreements from the officers, or possibly offering stock options before closing the deal. It's all a way to tie people to the company, to make people feel that everybody has benefited from this deal—the buyer, the seller, the employees.

♦ If you export, you are likely to find that consumers in foreign markets are more demanding than those at home. What attitude do you and your staff have toward constructive criticism of your product or service?

No matter what type of growth you pursue and how well you plan for it, no expansion ever turns out exactly the way you think it will. Besides being committed to growth, is your management also willing to bend a little? If your team is too rigid, it may break your chances of success.

7. Capacity.   It is fine to say that you want to grow. But can you really deliver to your customers? Answering the following questions will help you determine whether you have the operational resources you need in order to grow without going under and, if you need to increase your capacity, whether it's worth the potential cost.

♦ Are you meeting demand for your products in current markets? If so, do you have the plant capacity to produce for new markets?

♦ What is the state of your plant and equipment? Are they in good condition? Do they need repair? Are they state of the art?

♦ Will adding capacity to meet increased demand, in fact, be counterproductive? Some products and some expansions lend themselves well to economies of scale. Others don't—doubling sales just means doubling costs, or more. Is your technology easily and economically transferrable? Or is the technology so expensive that once you reach capacity you have to start again with a whole new plant?

Take the example of a company that manufactures fiberglass insulation. Once it reaches capacity, making the next bat of insulation can cost millions of dollars because the company has to build an entire new plant, complete with new furnaces, to fill that order. You can say that you want to expand worldwide, but once you get to a certain level, it might not make economic sense. Some businesses simply are not that easy to expand.

♦ Do you have the capacity to source enough raw materials? Is the worldwide supply of materials you need diminishing or becoming prohibitively expensive or difficult to access? Is the current level of quality of your materials changing? Will any of these factors inhibit your expansion?

♦ Do you have the computer systems and expertise to cope with more orders, more inventory, new shipping and delivery demands?

8. Time and patience.   It takes longer for some types of expansion to produce results—and profitability—than others. Growth through acquisition, for example, is usually faster than growth through exporting. Nonetheless, all growth requires the resources of time and patience. Do you and your company have them?

♦ Do you, your senior employees, the company's directors, and shareholders have the time and patience to wait for the long-term financial results that you expect from the expansion? As noted earlier, below normal profits for a period may mean some belt-tightening is in order. Shareholders may see the value of their shares remain stable or even drop. How long will they wait for share prices to rise or for dividends to be paid again?

♦ How long can you expect management to go through the process of expansion before it sees results? Does your management team see integration of a purchased or merged company as one of its prime responsibilities?

♦ If you have long-term plans for expansion, is your management team prepared to be constantly putting out fires as well as pursuing its normal duties?

♦ Depending on how you expand, how will your employees react to continuous upheaval as you grow, add new staff, and enter new markets? Have they the patience to accommodate the change, knowing that things will "settle down" eventually, either when you stop growing and take a breather, or when expansion, and all the change that comes with it, becomes second nature and simply part of the job?

♦ Do your bankers and other lenders have the patience to wait out your expansion for improved profits? Will they get nervous if you can't turn things around in short order? Some companies expand and are profitable almost immediately. Others need a year or two to digest, rationalize, and develop a stronger, larger, more profitable enterprise. How will your lenders react to what could be perceived as a sea of red ink as you buy up competitors or develop new markets? Never forget that bankers are lenders, not venture capitalists. They want their loans to be repaid on time and interest to be paid promptly when due. And the larger their loans, the more they want to know about you, your expansion plans, and what kind of progress you are making.

♦ Do your suppliers and customers have the patience to wait out the upheaval that comes with some types of expansion? Getting bigger may mean introducing new computer systems, a new distribution network, and perhaps even a series of new, improved products. It could mean a name change, a change in your corporate culture, and it most likely will mean a change in people. Your suppliers and customers might see a higher than normal turnover of the people they have become accustomed to dealing with, simply because internal promotions are coming fast and furious as you expand. Both suppliers and customers can get nervous if they perceive too much change too quickly, unless you show them that the expansion and resulting change benefits them directly.

♦ Finally, do you have the patience to stop, sit back, and digest the expansion you have just undertaken? Growing too fast is dangerous. Every type of expansion needs to be integrated with the whole, and that takes time. No matter how well you have planned, you have to take time out for stabilization—a breather from the constant drive to grow and dominate. Not every expansion goes exactly according to plan or works out exactly as you expected. If you continue to expand, problems may go unsolved, integration isn't completed, and your next round of expansion may suffer accordingly.

Assessing the Risk

Now that you have assessed your resources, you also need to assess the risk that growth entails and your readiness to assume that risk. Are you willing to put your existing business at risk in order to expand? Answering this question is a must before you go ahead.

In 1987, before merging with Premdor, Century faced this question when we became interested in making our first U.S. acquisition. In order to secure financing for the deal, we had to put up Century's Canadian assets as security. It was a risk, and we could have lost everything if the acquisition hadn't worked out. But it was a calculated risk, based on our knowledge of the economy, the door industry, and the resources of our Canadian company. We managed the risk and won.

It's true that you have to take risks to be successful. But those who are most successful know how to minimize their risk. You can buy a hemorrhaging company at a good price and turn it around. Or you can pay more and buy a company that has been successful for the last 25 years. You control the risk by the kind of company you buy. You can grow slowly by adding one product at a time to your line or you can go all out and add ten at once. You can expand by entering markets close to home or you can leap into markets across the country or across the ocean. You can watch the downside, know the risk, and control it to the best extent possible, or you can take a flyer.

You also can push a bad growth decision, taking the chance that the success and luck you have enjoyed in the past will continue. Or you can be honest with yourself and admit that something is wrong. Being realistic is part of controlling risk.

Notwithstanding what you've just read, you're likely to have a gut feeling about whether growth is worth the risk. If you have a good understanding of all the factors that can affect your proposed expansion and you listen to your intuition when making your decision, chances are that you'll be alright.

Putting the Plan on Paper

If you think you have what it takes to grow without going under, get serious and put it in writing. Planning your expansion should be a formal process. Talk is cheap; sitting at a table and discussing ideas isn't enough. It is essential that your ideas be committed to paper. The elements of a good business plan are discussed in more detail in Chapter 2.

Drawing up an organizational chart also should be part of your planning process. It will help you identify your strengths and weaknesses. The best way to do your chart is to draw what your organization *should* look like and compare this with what your organization *does* look like. Chances are you will either end up with a number of empty boxes or with too many people for too few boxes. If you already have twenty people who report to the president, maybe you have a weakness—you can't really add another ten if you merge or make an acquisition.

Making the Commitment to Change

The purpose of this chapter is to help you determine both whether you want to expand and whether you should expand. If you are still up for expansion, then read on. If you're not, you're still ahead of the game. You've made your decision, and you know where to concentrate your efforts. And that means you've got as much out of this chapter as someone who is ready to read the rest of the book.

If you do decide not to expand, or at least not to expand right now, keep one vitally important thing in mind: Today, no company can afford to stand still. Trade barriers such as tariffs, duties, and regulations to protect domestic producers are coming down around the world and will continue to do so throughout this decade. Therefore, even if you are not ready to expand in order to meet new challenges, you must be ready to change.

Look around. Are your competitors expanding? If so, they will soon have advantages, such as economies of scale or reduced cyclical impact on their businesses, that you won't have. If you are going to stay small in an industry in which everyone else is growing, planning is still paramount. Plan to become a niche player. There are plenty of success stories of companies that have done just that and have done extremely well.

In the final analysis, the message is the same for small companies, large companies, and growing companies—don't just keep doing what you've always done; get busy planning for change.

CHAPTER 2

Planning Your Financing

This chapter raises key questions about the cost of growth, including:

♦ Do you have sufficient financial information to grow?

♦ How will expansion affect the financing of your existing business?

♦ How can you account for *all* the costs of growth?

♦ What are your financing options?

Financing Fundamentals

Taking stock of your financial resources is the second essential step in assessing whether your company has what it takes to grow. At this point, you already have an idea of whether it makes sense for your company to pursue growth as a major corporate objective. And you also have an idea of whether your company has sufficient knowledge, flexibility, capacity, and time to handle growth well. Now you must determine whether you have the financial strength to go ahead.

Financial strength is made up of a number of elements, but the most important is a strong balance sheet with sufficient equity to finance expansion. At its very core, financial strength also includes good financial information systems, without which meaningful business plans and expansion plans cannot be drawn up, progress cannot be tracked, and timely adjustments cannot be made. In short, without good financial reporting systems, growth cannot be controlled.

As you might note, such factors often were not included in 1980s-style descriptions of financial resources, if indeed, financial resources were even defined in the 1980s as anything other than the ability to borrow. In the 1990s, however, there has been a turnaround in thinking about the best ways to finance growth. Whether you agree with the 1990s attitude is also an integral part of your company's financial resources and its ability to grow without going under. Some characteristic features of 1980s- and 1990s-style growth are compared in Figure 2-1.

Your Planning Is Only as Good as Your Information

As was mentioned in Chapter 1, there are certain basic elements or core resources that must exist in your company before you can successfully expand. Good financial reporting is one of them. If you don't have internal systems to gather and report financial information on a timely basis, you won't be able to produce realistic estimates of the cost of expansion. And if you don't know all the costs, you will eventually lose control of your growth. Even if you have good internal accounting procedures, you won't be able to come up with realistic projections if you don't know how to effectively use the information your system produces.

When you are planning an expansion, your external accountants and other advisors can help with some aspects of your proposed expansion. In particular, they can help you with tax planning. Any expansion you undertake will have tax implications, so it is important to get professional advice

---

Figure 2-1. How has the climate for growth changed?

1980s	1990s
◆ Abundance of financing.	◆ Tight money as lenders pull in horns.
◆ Raise debt.	◆ Raise equity.
◆ Race to fast growth.	◆ Emphasis on steady, planned growth.
◆ Diversification.	◆ Growth focused within own industry.
◆ Spotlight on percentage of sales growth.	◆ Concentration on profit, market share, and return on equity.
◆ Add new customers.	◆ Build strategic relations with existing customers.
◆ Try anything.	◆ Build on strengths/know thyself.

in this area. However, outside professionals provide only static information at a particular point in time. It is essential for you and your team to:

♦ Look at your business dynamically, on an ongoing basis.

♦ Look at variables and determine how they will affect your company, not just how, in theory, they might affect "Company X" in a hypothetical economic setting.

♦ Look at the relationships between particular actions and costs.

Suppose, for example, that you have a plant with excess capacity. You find that by adding $1 million of volume a year at that plant, your costs per unit are reduced because you are absorbing more overhead and more labor. What alternatives does this give you for expansion? For one thing, it could mean that exporting is more viable than you thought. By assuming that overheads are already being absorbed with domestic production, you can begin to justify and overcome the additional costs of exporting, such as freight, warehousing, and sales costs. This may mean that you end up with a competitive advantage as you enter the new export market, or you may discover that you can direct a larger portion of the budget to advertising in the new market. On the other hand, since your overall costs per unit have declined as a result of exporting, you may be able to reduce domestic prices. You might then gain a larger market share and thus begin using even more of your excess capacity to meet increased demand.

From the time you begin to develop your expansion plan, through the implementation stage, and on to the successful operation of your larger company, daily attention to and regular analysis of timely financial information will give you increased insight into the immediate and potential effects of taking certain actions and following certain strategies. Thus, it is critical to have in place the financial reporting systems that will enable you to both plan and monitor your expansion. And it is critical that you make adequate use of the information your systems provide. Information is power. Good financial information and the control that comes with it are absolutely essential to sound, successful growth of any type.

Developing Your Business Plan

Successful expansion plans grow out of good business plans. With a fully integrated financial reporting package, you have the resources to develop a business plan for your growth. This is a must, no matter what type of expansion you undertake.

Don't forget that while you are developing your business plan now to determine costs and financing needs, the real value of the plan is in its future use as a model against which to measure performance. In that sense, your business plan is a navigational chart. First, you need the proper information in order to chart your course. As you go, you need continuing, accurate input in order to keep your bearings and stay on course so that you arrive at your destination as predicted. If you don't have good financial reporting, you won't know with any certainty whether you're on course or drifting. To track your long-term progress, it is also imperative to constantly compare actual results to budgets and previous years' results. That is why, on its own, without continual corroboration, a good business plan is really no good at all.

Of course, if you will be appealing to outside investors to become involved with your expansion or you will be going to the bank for additional financing, a business plan is essential. These parties want to know as much as possible about you, your business, and your plans so they can assess the risk that goes along with any commitment to financing.

A good business plan has three main elements:

1. A narrative documentation of objectives, strategy, and assumptions.

2. Financial analysis, including an income statement, balance sheet, and cash flow projections.

3. Sensitivity analysis.

Narrative

Contrary to what many people think, the most important element in a good business plan is *not* the budget and projected income, although, as already noted, the financial information in the plan clearly must be sound. The most important element of a good business plan is a narrative description of your objectives, strategy, assumptions, and timetable for accomplishing your objectives. Some key questions your narrative should address include:

- ◆ Why is the particular type of expansion being considered appropriate? How will the company benefit from it?

- ◆ Is this type of expansion logical given other corporate goals?

- ◆ Why is the timing right for this particular growth step?

- ◆ What effects will expansion have on the company and its core resources, including management, staff, production, and financing? How will these effects be managed?

- ◆ Why is expansion worth the cost?

Objectives.   In the objectives section of your business plan, you should identify and evaluate targets and opportunities. Those that meet your company's criteria for further investigation you should discuss in greater detail and then give reasons for focusing on the one or two objectives you have chosen.

Strategies.   Showing that your strategies are sound requires that you demonstrate very clearly, step by step, how and why you will achieve the dollar volume you expect to in sales. If you are entering a new market, how do you intend to take market share away from the current participants in that market? Will you enter with an acquisition? Is your product or service lower priced but of similar quality so that you will be able to compete successfully on price? How long will you be able to sustain a price advantage? Have you taken account of all barriers to entry in a particular market, such as your potential customers' commitment to purchasing locally produced goods or services, market saturation, or a distribution system peculiar to the market that you may not be able to gain access to?

When Premdor enters a new market, we do enough research to determine how virtually all doors are sold in that market. If we don't know enough, we go back and do more research. When we entered the French market by acquiring a door manufacturer in Bordeaux in 1993, we knew that the existing sales of this company would allow us to introduce new and less expensive products into the French market, particularly moulded-panel residential doors. We then evaluated the distribution network in France and, for one segment, determined that we had to develop strategic alliances with at least two of the largest distributors. Our strategies were thoroughly researched and very specifically laid out in our expansion plan and, we feel as a consequence, our objectives were met on or ahead of schedule.

Assumptions.   Your expansion objectives and strategies are only as good as the assumptions on which they are based. And those assumptions must be reasonable and sound. Economic assumptions pose little trouble except for gathering the appropriate information. Industry statistics and trends may be more difficult to unearth and, in many cases, may not be as well founded as general economic assumptions. Much more problematic are the assumptions you make about how your operation fits into your industry and your markets and how you compare to your competition.

As you develop the assumptions you need to construct a comprehensive business plan, you must answer questions such as:

◆ What is the economic outlook for your market? This includes obtaining buyer and supplier data for your industry.

◇ Will the buyers of your product or service continue to have the same purchasing power as they have had in the past? Or is that purchasing power declining, or perhaps increasing?

◇ Is your entire industry, or are your immediate competitors, facing higher or lower costs over the coming years? Is the price of raw materials likely to increase dramatically? Is the cost of financing likely to drop, or will you experience sudden hikes in interest rates?

◇ Is it likely that you and your competitors and/or your buyers will be looking at increased government regulation now, or in the near future, that will affect your ability to supply product or services or your buyer's ability to acquire your product or services?

◇ Are there particular economic indicators that might signal a trend in future demand for your product or service? One of a number of indicators that Premdor uses is current and anticipated housing starts, a statistic supplied by the governments of most industrialized countries. Of course, other economic indicators are used by the statisticians to predict housing starts, and we also use those to predict future sales.

♦ Based on key indicators for your industry and economic indicators such as interest rates or currency exchange rates, why do you think your sales will be higher or lower?

◇ Are potential buyers still interested in your product or service? Or is a new alternative about to break into the marketplace and affect your anticipated growth? How likely is it that alternative, competitive products will enter the market over the time frame of your business plan?

◇ Are the market conditions that you face the same as those facing your competitors? Do some of them have access to lower-cost financing or cheaper labor? Can they use excess capacity to gain market share while you are currently using all your capacity and will find producing more product incrementally expensive?

♦ Will you be building market share? And if so, how will you be taking that market share away from your competitors? Or will you be selling a different product that promises to take market share away from your competitors?

♦ Have you lost some competition? Over the past few years, many companies have gone out of business, which in normal times would open up opportunities for those remaining in the market. However, if demand has shrunk at the same time, your expectations of picking up market slack may not be met.

♦ Are you adding new products? How will those new products fair against competing products? Will you be creating demand because the product is essentially new or significantly different enough from existing products? If so, on what are you basing future sales?

Timetable.   Any timetable that you commit to paper must be realistic in relation to your objectives, strategies chosen, and the assumptions made. If you are introducing a new product to a new market, you can't expect to garner a 50 percent share in six months if competition is fierce and the economy is still in the doldrums. Yes, "miracles" do occasionally happen. A new piece of software will take the high-tech market by storm in a matter of months. Or a new product will completely displace an established product over a short period of time. But these are the exceptions, not the rule. What you want in your business plan is an achievable timetable that makes sense considering your financing, your market, your competition, the economic environment, and a host of other factors. Reaching your goals months or even years ahead of target will bring kudos—missing your goals by many months or even years could seriously jeopardize your business, especially if it spells the departure of your investors and/or bankers. Don't succumb to excessive optimism.

The Importance of Narrative Before Numbers.   Your management team may balk at the exercise of composing a narrative business plan. After all, it is a lot of work and demands a great deal of clear thinking and organization. But insist on it: No numbers and no budgets allowed until you have a descriptive business plan. The type of questions just outlined, and many more, should be answered first and turned into a coherent narrative before a single production or sales number is introduced to the process. Why? Because budgeting gives people an excuse to take last year's figures, enter them in the computer, and add 5 percent to arrive at this year's projected budget. That is an accounting exercise, not a planning exercise—it doesn't make people think.

Committing ideas to paper is more difficult than budgeting. It forces you and your management team to examine your ideas in a clear and detailed fashion. This may mean that you change the plan as you go along, but that is what the decision-making process is about. Committing a plan to paper leaves a permanent trail. It acts as a benchmark against which to measure progress. And it helps you devise implementation schedules, outlining an orderly sequence of where you want to go, why, and approximately when you hope to get there. It forces you to sort through options and set priorities, both short-term and long-term. If selling in Europe is one of your ultimate goals, you can and should identify that growth step ahead of time as long as you recognize that other steps will likely have to come first.

Premdor's approach has always been one of stepped growth. We take a step up and then stop for a while until everything in our organization rises to the new level. Only then do we take another step up.

In 1989, for example, when Premdor and Century merged, the company created was twice as large in size, making us one of North America's premier manufacturers and distributors of doors. We waited until 1991 to take our next major growth step, acquiring three U.S. door companies. We then spent an entire year integrating the new companies, bringing together senior management, rationalizing operations, and retiring debt. It was only when we were completely comfortable in our new skin as a larger company that we felt we could take another step, purchasing a door company in California and another in Texas in 1992.

While we had been exporting to Europe since 1983, one of our strategic objectives was to eventually establish more of a presence there. Early in 1993, we made our move, acquiring a door manufacturing company in France. Along the way, we have identified a number of other growth steps that we want to take. And we will take them. But not until we are sure that we're ready.

Financial Analysis

Your narrative should be followed up with a financial analysis that is, essentially, a numerical representation of your objectives and assumptions. It is always tempting to see your forecast income as the most important part of your financial analysis, but beware of neglecting your balance sheet and projected cash flow. They are critical to successfully planning your financing.

Every dollar of growth requires a corresponding amount of working capital. So, if you are planning to expand, especially rapidly, say through an acquisition, you need to know how you will finance the operations of your instantly larger company. Will you need more equity? Will you need to take on more debt? Don't be lulled into thinking that if you have the equity, or the bank is lending you the money to buy a company, you can worry about the operations later. You need detailed planning.

Growth demands financing for new plant and equipment, personnel, advertising, research and development, and a host of other one-time or ongoing expenses. Also, every dollar of growth means a corresponding amount of growth in your accounts receivable and inventory. And that means your financing or equity has to accommodate this side of growth, too. Unless you know how much your financing has to grow, you will be in trouble even though you have the other expenses of growth covered. That's why companies can go under faster by growing too fast or without control— not every financing detail is taken care of or accounted for in advance; speed often means that details are swept under the rug and forgotten.

You should be able to break down every dollar of growth into the corresponding dollar amount of equity or debt financing required to finance it. For example, say your receivables turn every 30 days. If you sell someone a dollar of goods at the beginning of the month, you will have that dollar in accounts receivable for a month. Part of your receivables may be financed by your payables, but much if not all of those accounts receivable have to be financed either by equity or by debt. And that financing has to be figured in as part of your expansion financing. It won't just take care of itself.

E very business can come up with an appropriate financing expansion ratio. Premdor has made a point of doing this. We know what additional financing is required for every increase of a dollar in sales. The ratio changes from time to time as we grow. But, as mentioned earlier, one of our strategic objectives is to expand. Thus, the financing expansion ratio is as central to our operations as any other traditional financial ratio.

In addition to determining financing needs, expansion also means that the financial side of your business will take on a different look. You may have been making stable profits up to this point, but if you are heading into an expansion, that will very likely change. Your company will need more working capital. You may bump up against the upper limit of your line of credit for the first time in your company's history. You might have to look at new ways of financing—perhaps different kinds of debt or new equity. Remuneration of senior people may change. Long-term incentives may be implemented. And certainly, shareholders should be prepared to receive less in dividends during the expansion phase. Indeed, in most cases, companies that are taking a fairly large growth step shouldn't even pay dividends, but should keep their resources inside the business.

Preparing to make this financial commitment is part and parcel of the fact that, throughout a period of expansion, there is a tendency to take a small step back in order to go forward. Understanding that progress does not necessarily mean constantly moving forward is part of understanding the expansion process.

Sensitivity Analysis

When you expand, you can count on nothing going exactly as planned and everything taking longer than your best guess. That's why it is important to perform a sensitivity analysis on your business plan. By running your plan through different scenarios—including changes in interest rates, changes in pricing structures, or slower-than-expected sales, for example—you will have an idea, in advance, of how certain variables will affect you and how you can adapt. You will be able to establish a range within which your plan is viable. And working within that range means that you will maintain control over your expansion process.

Computers have made planning and performing sensitivity analysis much easier than in the past. For example, it's now easy to find out how lowering your gross profit margin by 3 percent would affect the bottom line or how fluctuations in exchange rates would affect your cash flow if you were to export. But the fact that computers make modeling easy doesn't mean that the task is actually performed with regularity in most companies or that enough attention is paid to the results.

It sounds like plain common sense to run your sensitivity analyses and pay attention to the results. It also sounds like plain common sense to have good reporting systems in place that produce more than just good year-end statements. After all, armed with a good plan and sound, accurate, and timely information, you should have plenty of forewarning and time to correct for problems or changing circumstances as you go along. Yet it is surprising how few North American companies have good systems, good reporting, and good forecasting, and also have the good sense to pay attention to their information.

What Does It Cost to Expand?

That question has as many answers as there are types of expansion.

For example, the cost of expanding into a new market can be very different depending on the strategy used to enter the market. Suppose your company is based in Massachusetts and you want to begin dealing in Texas. Suppose also that you can expand either by starting up a new operation there or by acquiring an existing player. Depending on which strategy you choose, there will be a difference in the way your competitors in Texas react. And those reactions will affect your game plan and your costs.

If you were to start up a new operation in Texas, you would be adding capacity to the existing market there. This means you would have to sell that capacity, and this might be difficult. Competition with other companies would be intense, and this of course could affect profitability. Would it still be worthwhile to pursue your expansion plan?

Then suppose you could expand into Texas by acquiring an existing player there. You would not immediately be adding capacity, and this could affect profitability also, at least in the short term.

Start-Ups

In a case such as the previous one, not only is the cost of a start-up quite different from that of an acquisition, but the ultimate cost of the start-up is also much more difficult to determine. Therefore, in drawing up the income statement, balance sheet, and cash flow projections for a start-up, it pays to be very conservative. In fact, since few start-ups make money in the first year, it's wise to budget for a loss. It's also essential to calculate what effect your start-up investment, and the initial lack of return on it, will have on your existing business.

♦ What will happen if sales in the new market are slower than forecast?

♦ What if your new operations don't make a profit for a number of years?

♦ Will you be drawing more heavily on your lines of credit? Are your lines of credit sufficient to support this?

Also, don't forget that neglecting to do your homework can be very costly. What would happen to your existing business if you made the mistake of creating new capacity in a market that already is oversupplied?

Acquisitions

While the purchase price is the most obvious cost of acquiring another company in your own industry, there may be after-acquisition costs related to the new, combined entity, and these have to be figured into the total cost of this type of growth. If you buy a company that has been undercapitalized, for example, you may subsequently find that an injection of capital, equity, or financing is required to get operations running smoothly. Thus, an integral part of planning financing for an acquisition involves looking beyond the initial purchase price of the target company and determining what the ongoing financial needs of the combined entity will be.

Mergers

The financing needs of a company that is the product of a merger will depend on the financial profile of the two companies tying the corporate knot. Typically, two companies bring their respective strengths to a merger and form a much larger company the whole of which is more than the sum of the two individual companies. In many cases, one of the partners brings strong financing to the new entity.

In some cases, however, two companies with relatively weak financing will merge in anticipation of forming a larger, stronger company that can compete more successfully in their particular industry. This larger company needs a more robust financial base if it is to survive, and typically it would need a stronger equity base. If the two merged companies simply rely on their current financing situation, they may not see an appreciable reduction in costs and may find themselves as uncompetitive as they were before the merger.

Internal Growth

Growing internally, say by adding product lines, demands less up-front financing than growing by acquisition or start-up. But bear in mind that your total estimate of the price tag for this type of growth must also include other costs—for example, the increased costs of financing a larger inventory.

Vertical Integration

Vertical integration simply means buying a business that is in your chain of production or distribution. You might buy up the chain, for example, by purchasing a retail operation or you might buy down the chain, perhaps acquiring a raw materials supplier. Whichever way you are thinking of going, you can be sure that there will be additional costs to your integration that are not immediately apparent.

If you integrate upward and buy out one of your major customers, for instance, that may strengthen your position in the market. But it will also put you in competition with your own customers. Premdor could expand by buying a chain of home improvement stores, but if we did, other home center chains probably wouldn't continue to buy our doors. Thus, the cost of integrating forward can be much more far-reaching than the initial financing needed to go into business as a distributor or retailer; the cost also includes the effect that your decision will have on your current customer base. In addition, integrating forward might also have an effect on your accounts receivable. Can you obtain the necessary financing that will be required to carry more receivables?

If you integrate back down the chain and, say, buy out a supplier who provides you with key components or raw materials, again, there will be more to your overall costs than buying the plant and equipment. Because you are dealing with another set of raw materials, your inventory levels will be affected, which in turn affects your financing. If the supplier that you intend to buy was supplying your competition, those contracts could dry up. The competition will look for new suppliers, and the purchase could prove to be uneconomical. Trying to anticipate the underlying costs of vertical integration is, therefore, crucial when you plan your financing.

Most importantly, if you expand up or down the production chain, you likely will be getting into a new business with which you're not familiar. Selling at retail is not the same as selling at wholesale, and digging or cutting raw materials isn't the same as fashioning them into finished goods. Are you fully aware of the costs of getting into this new business? Do you know how to run it successfully? Can it be integrated into your old business?

Horizontal Expansion

This type of expansion typified growth in the 1980s and, as we are witnessing in the 1990s, it's a difficult type of growth to undertake successfully. Many companies that diversified in the 1980s are now busy getting back to their knitting. They found that acquiring businesses in industries not related to their core business meant that customers, processes, and everything else about the business was also new to them, and they got into trouble.

This book is not about how to expand by getting into a new industry. It's about how to expand successfully in the industry you are in. Because horizontal expansion creates a new level of risk for your existing business and is difficult to control, it can be dangerous.

―――――――――――

One of the reasons that Premdor does well is that the company is extremely focused. Investors and business observers like our strategy of expanding while staying in the same business, although sticking to this philosophy in the 1980s made us feel somewhat like loners. Rather than staying in Canada and going from doors to windows to hardware to stair parts, and so on, we stayed in doors and went east, west, south, then to Europe, and on to the Pacific Rim. As mentioned earlier, the company performed well even at the worst of economic times. And we still haven't left doors.

Where Will You Get Your Financing?

You can't grow without money—there's nothing new in that. What is new in the 1990s is that attitudes about where to get money have changed fairly dramatically since the 1980s. Debt is out, equity is in and, these days, the less debt you have, the better off you'll be.

Equity Financing

What are the best sources for equity financing? If yours is a privately held company with a strong balance sheet and a strong capital base, you are your own best source of equity financing.

However, since the number of companies with deep pockets of their own is limited, and since some types of expansion can be far more costly than others, the idea of bringing in new money through attracting an operating partner or a private investor often makes sense. But at what price?

Active equity partners, such as venture capitalists, have recently been trying to reduce risk by investing in established companies that want to expand. In return, however, they often look for involvement in the day-to-day business, including involvement in decision making. Fear of loss of control can make some businesses shy away from this type of partnership. Nonactive investors will be more hands-off, investing money in the business and waiting in the wings for returns.

Virtually all investors, however, demand a certain degree of comfort about the industry in which they are about to invest. And all investors must be satisfied with the skill, dedication, and vision of management. In fact, many astute investors look no further than assessing the quality of management and the likelihood that the current management team will remain intact for the time the investor has money at risk in the company. The type of industry and the nature of the product or service sold is secondary to management's ability to perform successfully. A good salesperson can sell practically anything to almost anybody. Similarly, a quality management team can make virtually any business perform successfully. The most scarce and the most valuable resource in the marketplace is the combination of top-notch entrepreneurial and managerial ability.

Bear in mind that investors can be found in places that might not at first seem obvious. For example, if you have a product that you believe will do well in a new market and you also have a potential customer for the product, perhaps that customer would be willing to invest with you in the new market. Or, if a supplier saw that your expansion would mean more business for him, perhaps he might be willing to invest in your growth.

Mergers as a Source of Financing

Merging with another company also can provide a source of financing. In the classic situation, a company with a great product, great distribution, and which is expanding quickly, has cash flow problems. A more mature competitor, or perhaps a compatible business, has excess cash but does not have the products or distribution network to undertake any type of significant expansion. An acquisition doesn't really make sense since the excess cash will then have to be used to buy out the owners of the more aggressive business, leaving little for expansion. A merger allows each company to take advantage of the strengths of the other.

In most situations, the larger merged company will be looked on more favorably by the banks, assuming that it has not leveraged up its balance sheet. If the point of a merger is to secure financing and strengthen the two companies, it is important that the merger not drain any cash out of the combined companies. This may not always be possible, especially if some shareholders are anxious to get out and buying them out with excess cash is the only way to carry through with the merger. In any case, a merger should be looked on as one source of financing that ought to be compared with other alternatives.

Taking Your Company Public

In the aftermath of numerous failed 1980s partnerships, privately held companies are finding it more difficult to find investors in the 1990s. If you have a sound expansion plan but are unable to raise sufficient financing on your own and don't want to accumulate debt, you might consider taking your company public.

Public companies have opportunities in equity markets that just don't exist for private companies. For example, today, investors want liquidity. They want to be able to get in on an investment opportunity but they also want the ability to get out, even if the investment has done well. Public companies have the advantage of offering this liquidity.

When a privately held company considers going public, fear of giving up control is always an issue. If, like many debt averse companies in the 1990s, you are thinking of going the public route, you will have to grapple with certain questions:

♦ Is expansion important enough to the success of the business that you are willing to give up a potentially substantial amount of ownership? Once that ownership is given up, you won't get it back.

♦ On the other hand, is it better to own 40 percent of a business that is successful than to own 100 percent of a business that cannot grow?

When Premdor merged with Century in 1989, Premdor was a public company and Century was not. Under the terms of the merger, Century shareholders gave up 100 percent ownership of the private company and took back a 30 percent stake in the new, combined entity, which is public. Why did they do it? They did it because of the potential created by the merger. The ownership they gave up allowed them to gain ownership in a much larger, public company that offers much more opportunity. Today, there wouldn't be a shareholder who would say that he or she was disappointed in the trade-off that was made.

Four advantages offered by a public company, in particular, stand out:

1. There is access to capital markets. The ability to raise equity can be extremely important if your strategy includes expansion.

2. A public company is able to use its stock as currency. The market places an easily determinable value on the company's stock, and this stock can be used in lieu of cash in various transactions, including acquisitions.

3. The company typically gains an enormous amount of credibility. Through going public, a company's corporate image is strengthened and its competitive position will likely be enhanced. Public companies listed on a well-respected stock exchange gain a certain presence, nationally and internationally. This kind of recognition and credibility can be a big help in dealing with suppliers, customers, acquisition targets, and bankers.

4. Going public can help you attract, keep, and motivate key employees through meaningful stock option and share purchase plans.

Taking a company public can be arduous. There are many regulatory hoops through which you, your directors, your senior management, and the company will have to jump. Your internal reporting will likely have to be strengthened to support the public disclosure required of a public company. You will have to prepare for life in a fish bowl as your financial information will now be public. As well, your company may have to be restructured to conform to public company standards and regulatory requirements. However, a good brokerage firm can be a big help during the process, and a great many companies go public every year.

You will also have to choose the appropriate exchange on which to list. Premdor is listed on three exchanges. We are a Canadian company listed on the Toronto and Montreal exchanges. And, in 1993, we also listed on the New York Stock Exchange.

By the end of 1992, approximately 70 percent of Premdor's revenues, plants, and people were located in the United States. As a result, we felt it was a sound and a responsible strategy to expand the capital markets in which Premdor's stock is traded. It would reflect the commitment the company has to doing business in the United States.

Also, increasing the shareholder base, and therefore its liquidity, would increase value for both current and future shareholders. Adding up these factors, we decided to list on a senior U.S. stock exchange.

Premdor is a leader in our industry and is truly a North American company. In early January 1993, through an acquisition in France, we began the next stage in our development— becoming an international company. Based primarily on these factors, we concluded it was appropriate to list on the world's preeminent exchange, the New York Stock Exchange.

Once you go public, you and your senior management will have to face a number of realities—they are unavoidable and must be dealt with successfully:

1. Never forget that you are running the company for the benefit of *all* the shareholders, not just a few. This is easy to say, but you must be committed to that principle at all times.

2. Management must demonstrate a high degree of integrity. Investors have put their money at risk in your company. You must earn their trust every day.

3. There is a distinct difference between running the business and building investor relations. You will have to find a balance between the two, bearing in mind that your first priority is to run a successful company.

4. Carrying out your stated plans is critical in a public company. Do what you say you are going to do, which builds confidence. Investors don't like surprises.

5. Continue to build a solid management team, and develop a dependable and competent backup. Potential investors will look at your team closely.

6. If your company is to be successful, it must be followed by analysts. However, since they tend to think in terms of quarter to quarter,

you will have to balance the long-term goals of your corporate strategy with the short-term snapshots that are a part of public company analysis.

7. What goes up also goes down. Don't lose sight of the fact that you are responsible for improving shareholder value over the *long term*. This is your most important objective. Daily or weekly fluctuations in the price of the stock can be distracting, but you have to get used to it.

8. Surround yourself with the best professional advisors you can find and use them, and your board of directors, effectively. That's what you're paying them for.

9. Understand the regulatory environment in which you operate and *always* make the proper disclosures.

Running a public company is not for everyone. It means changing your focus. Many executives who were principal owners say, and initially believe, that they can commit themselves to the greater good of all the shareholders. But they may find it difficult to carry through on that commitment.

When you run a public company, you may have to make decisions that are unpopular in the short run, even though those decisions are good for the company in the long run. You may have one or two major shareholders, and it might be in their interest if the company paid dividends—but it may not be in the best long-term interest of the company. If you are not absolutely confident that you can make the difficult decisions and run the company for all the shareholders, you may want to reconsider going public.

Franchising

Franchising, which is discussed in more detail in Chapter 4, is essentially a means of expanding your business using other people's money. It enables you to establish outlets for your product or service without making an enormous capital investment.

In a franchise arrangement, you, as the franchisor, grant franchisees the right to use your corporate name and sell your product or service in an exclusive territory. Typically, you will also agree to provide your franchisees with national advertising support. In exchange, you receive an up-front, "buy-in" fee and royalties. You may also sell your franchisees, at a markup, certain materials, supplies, formulas, or technology specific to your business.

Franchising can be an effective way to expand and to raise money if you have the right kind of product or service. Witness McDonald's restaurants and hundreds of other retail operations across North America. It is also an effective strategy for expansion when times are tough and capital is scarce. However, maintaining control of the quality of the franchised product or service and satisfying franchisees that they are receiving value for their franchise royalties can be very difficult.

Government Assistance

Whether your company is public or private, don't overlook government assistance programs—at federal, state, or provincial levels—as possible sources for financing for your expansion. This is particularly true if you want to export. Governments in the United States and Canada are usually willing to encourage companies to develop exports by offering low-interest loans or nonrepayable loans. And every jurisdiction is anxious to help virtually any enterprise create employment in the area.

Debt Financing

If this book had been written in the 1980s, this section would have taken up almost the entire chapter. Now that it's the 1990s, the section will be considerably shorter. The most important thing to remember about using debt to finance your expansion is that it is very risky. Expansion itself creates risk. Expansion using a large dose of leverage creates even more risk. If you use your own money to finance growth, the worst outcome might be that you would lose all the money you've invested. If you use borrowed money to grow and you lose it, you will still have to find a way to pay that money back.

These days, even if you are tempted to expand on borrowed funds, you may not have much luck at the bank. Major lenders are smarting from loans that went bad during the recession, especially loans to megaborrowers whose financial troubles have reverberated throughout both the U.S. and Canadian banking industries.

Nonetheless, even companies with good track records are finding that the criteria for borrowing are much tighter in the 1990s than they were in the 1980s. Given their skittishness, the more you can do to reassure your bankers, the better off you'll be.

Bankers like to deal with clients who know how to borrow. Being such a client means that you don't expect your bankers to define your needs for you. Rather, you are prepared to tell your banker how much money you need. Don't make the grievous error of asking for less than you really require. By later exceeding a skimpy line of credit or having to come back to the bank for more financing sooner than expected, you put your management skills in doubt.

The ability to define your financing needs stems, of course, from good internal financial reporting and a sound business plan. Be prepared to back up your financing request with projections for the future, including operating and cash flow budgets, and the results of your sensitivity analyses. Some discussion of the outlook for your industry, your competitors, your products, and your management history and continuity are also important.

One area that is new to lending in the 1990s is the environmental "health" of borrowers. It is now absolutely necessary to provide your banker with assurances that your company is clean and "green" and does not represent an environmental risk. In the 1980s, many banks were surprised to discover that, on foreclosing on mortgages or other debts, they had become the proud owners of an environmental disaster from which the former owners were walking away. The banks learned quickly and now demand an environmental audit if they see your company and/or industry posing any kind of environmental risk. This includes operating on land or in a building that may pose a risk generated by its former owners.

Lenders want to know two essential things:

1. Will any security registered on your property, such as a mortgage, be worth what it is stated to be worth? If environmental problems, past, present, or future, jeopardize that security in any way, the lender will likely look for other types of security.

2. Will you be put out of business by environmental problems at any time in the future? Will cleanup costs or other costs of compliance put you under?

Lenders now want to see an environmental management plan from virtually any company that they think poses any type of environmental risk.

It's worth noting that paying off your loan is not necessarily the most important aspect of your relationship with your banker. Bankers want predictability. They want to be serviced regularly. Think of them as your suppliers, not as your business partners. Like any prudent supplier, bankers want to minimize risk and, at the same time, be assured of making a reasonable profit. And they don't want surprises. Therefore, keep your banker happy by doing what you have said you would do, making payments on time, and abiding by the covenants in your loan agreement.

Private Debt

Private debt financing could be just as difficult or more difficult to secure than bank financing. Institutional investors usually are not that interested in lending to smaller companies for expansion purposes, particularly if they are private companies.

However, you may have more luck with the so-called merchant bankers or mezzanine financiers. They are more interested in situations with a higher risk than the banks are, and they are certainly more creative when it comes to developing a debt package that you can live with. Yes, interest rates will typically be higher than those offered by the banks, and merchant bankers often will want equity. There is no standard type of mezzanine financing deal. Since each one tends to be written up based on the particular situation, it is critical that you review any such arrangement carefully with your professional advisers.

Expansion at What Price?

Doing business in the 1990s isn't like doing business in the 1980s. While you still have to spend money to make money, the difference is that now you have to *have* the money to spend; it's unwise to borrow it. Therefore, the critical question to answer when planning your financing for expansion is do you have a sufficient capital base? Undercapitalization is the surest way to undermine an expansion plan. If your capital base is not sufficient to support expansion, you will grow yourself out of business.

Your financial equation, then, rests on this: Is the opportunity created by expansion so great that it is worth giving up some ownership or taking in a partner-investor or creating additional debt on the books to take advantage of that opportunity? Or, would you rather carry on business at your current size, bearing in mind that, as noted in the last chapter, in order to maintain a competitive advantage, you will have to be ready and willing to accommodate change in your present market?

PART TWO
Expanding at Home

CHAPTER 3

Expanding Internally: Getting More from Your Markets

This chapter covers the process of internal expansion through:

◆ Creating value for your customers.

◆ Improving your marketing.

◆ Extending product lines or adding new ones.

The Best Defense Includes a Good Offense

These days, companies choosing to catch the global wave and grow must mount a two-pronged strategy of:

1   Putting up a strong defense.

2. Developing a good offense.

It is imperative to develop a defensive strategy to protect your position in your domestic market. Don't confuse protecting what you've got with maintaining the status quo or standing still. Developing an effective defense means strengthening your position through internal growth. This can be accomplished by, for instance, paying close attention to your customers' needs, improving your marketing, adding new products or services to your lines, or opening more locations in your existing markets—in other words, giving your customers more reasons to buy from you and working to ensure that they never question why they are dealing with you.

This defense lays the foundation upon which you can build your offense—moving into new markets, strategies for which are discussed in later chapters.

Are You Ready to Expand Internally?

In developing your defense, your aim is to ensure that your business is competitive. Thus, taking stock of your present situation and capabilities is a critical first step. While you should go back and review the core resources outlined in Chapter 1, you should also ask yourself the questions outlined in Figure 3-1 in order to determine the strengths and weaknesses of your current defensive position.

Technology and Quality

The technological revolution is taking place in all types of industries. Computer technology and electronics are helping to create better quality products, and the goal of business is to have the most efficient operations possible. If that means investing in technology as part of a solid defense, then, that's what businesses must do. If a competitor 30 miles, 300 miles, or 3,000 miles away is employing technology to make a better-quality, lower-priced product and you are not using the same or better technology, you won't be able to compete over the long run.

Materials and Employees

Another key defensive move in the new competitive environment is striving to be a low-cost producer—survival depends on it. That means sourcing

---

Figure 3-1. Defense strengths and weaknesses checklist.

	Yes	No
1. Is my operation efficient? Have I kept up with technology and am I a low-cost producer?	☐	☐
2. Is the quality of my products sufficient?	☐	☐
3. Am I sourcing raw materials and services at the best possible prices?	☐	☐
4. Am I making the most effective use of my employees?	☐	☐
5. Is the company adequately financed so that it can take advantage of opportunities?	☐	☐
6. Are my marketing and sales efforts properly directed?	☐	☐

your raw materials at the best price and obtaining services at the best price. Since size gives you more clout with suppliers, this is one of the obvious benefits of pursuing growth.

While Premdor continually strives to increase sales worldwide, the company also concentrates on improving profit margins both through better utilization of fixed cost components and ongoing cost reduction programs.

Since raw materials account for a significant part of the cost of a typical hollow core wood door, one of our main objectives is to reduce the cost of raw materials through better pricing and new sources of supply. We have also been able to reduce the cost of certain materials by centralizing and consolidating our purchasing and making better use of inventory control systems. In addition, Premdor has successfully used alternative materials or substituted certain lower-cost materials while meeting or exceeding industry quality standards. During periods of rapidly escalating costs for certain materials such as the door industry experienced during 1993, such substitutions have become increasingly important for the company's bottom line.

Being a low-cost producer also means obtaining labor at the best price. Bear in mind, however, that the best price is not necessarily the cheapest price. In comparing labor costs, it's not enough to look at just hourly wages. Some plants pay higher wages than others in the same industry but are more successful. They have higher productivity, a better-trained workforce, lower absenteeism, and less turnover. They also have better facilities, appropriate technology, and have found better suppliers. Labor rates will affect your ability to compete in the new environment. But those rates must be effective in order for your defensive strategy to be effective.

The bottom line in becoming a low-cost producer is controlling your cost per unit. Concentrating on this objective is an important part of successful growth.

Financing

As discussed in the preceding chapter, your company has to be on sound financial ground to support expansion. If you are heavily leveraged, you won't have the flexibility and, in many cases, the time or patience, to wait for long-term results. If your financial resources are stretched, you may not be able to carry the increased inventory that is needed to meet increased sales or pay the extra freight to ship your products to new markets. In other words, if you are not adequately financed, you will lose control of your expansion.

Marketing and Sales

Anyone who sells anything can sell more through improved marketing. Staying close to your customers and demonstrating to them that your proximity means better service is a basic defensive tactic. So is adding products or services to your present line, thus giving customers more reason to buy from you. Improving your marketing to improve your market share is discussed in more detail later in this chapter.

Don't forget that if a beefed-up sales force or product line means beefed-up sales, it also means you'll need more capacity to produce, store, and deliver your goods or services.

How Do Your Competitors Stack Up?

Eventually, you must also assess your competitors' strengths and weaknesses in the previous areas. By doing so, you will be able to develop a plan for internal growth based on taking market share from them by exploiting your strengths and playing on their weaknesses. In large part, your competitive edge will also come from:

◆ Gathering more information than your competitors about your industry (making knowledge your business).

◆ Knowing more than your competitors about customer needs and the types of products and services the market seeks (knowing your customers' needs).

◆ Identifying what the end-user wants from products, and backing those needs through to the product you make or the service you deliver (creating value).

First, however, it is essential to evaluate how well you currently know your customers' needs.

Know Your Customers' Needs

For the moment, one of the most important steps you can take in planning your internal expansion is to stop thinking about both your own business and your competitors' business. If your focus is too inward, your defensive strategy will be defined by what you want, not by what the market wants. If your focus is too much on your competitors, your strategy will be defined on their terms. At some point you will have to test your strategy against the competition, but their actions should not be the starting point for your plans.

Instead, start thinking about your customers' business and your customers' needs. Do you know your customers well enough to answer these two key questions:

1. What do my customers need in a changing business environment?

2. Why should my customers buy from me instead of from anyone else?

Surprisingly, not many companies ask, or answer, these basic questions. If they did, more would grow. North American car makers are a prime example. During the seventies and eighties, the needs of car buyers shifted gears. In the showrooms and on the car lots, they started to look for either value or high quality, or a combination of value and high quality. North American car manufacturers delivered neither. Their low-end cars were bottom-of-the-barrel quality and therefore did not represent value, and their high-end cars were not high quality enough. Japanese car makers, on the other hand, worked to progressively know and satisfy consumers' changing needs, whether those needs were for dependability at the low end or dependable luxury at the high end.

In the 1990s, consumers are looking for price and value. Some retailers have responded to those needs by offering shoppers an incredible number of products at low prices in warehouse-style shopping locations. The Home Depot, a U.S. chain of home improvement centers, is one example. Currently, the home improvement industry is one of the fastest-growing industries in North America. Yet other players are falling by the wayside as Home Depot prospers. How has the company been so successful? By anticipating and responding to consumers' needs. In the process, it has reshaped the do-it-yourself supply business.

Rethink Your Business

As the previous examples illustrate, thinking about and delivering what customers want often means that a company must change the way it does business. And change is never easy. It may mean rethinking your products, rethinking how customers use them, and rethinking how to best organize your operations. Thus your growth strategy must be defined in terms of how to best serve your customers and create value for them, not in terms of how it's easiest to run your business or what strategies your competitors are using.

Look again at the American car makers. For them, finally listening to their customers' demands for value and quality has meant, essentially, redefining their business. Compare their current "quality is job #1" mantra to their former mission—churning out large numbers of cars that would be replaced every three years. The corporate strategy then was production oriented not value oriented. The attitude was "quantity over quality" and "make it now, fix it later."

This classic, and outmoded, mind-set isn't just typical of the North American auto industry. Look at the computer business and the electronics industry in North America. Why have the companies that dominated these industries in the 1960s and 1970s now lost market share to both home-grown and foreign competitors? Because their focus has been turned inward rather than outward toward their customers and their customers' changing demands.

It is clear that, today, determining your customers' needs, and developing an almost intimate knowledge of their business, is as big a part of your job as selling your product or service. And it's an integral part of an effective internal growth strategy.

F or Premdor, knowing our customers' business has meant thinking in terms of a "sell-through." We don't only sell *to* our customers (who are wholesale and retail building supply centers) because they are not the final users of our products. Their customers are the final users of our doors and mouldings. So, we sell our products *through* our customers to their customers. Thus, we have to know not only our own business but also our customers' business, and we have to be consumer oriented.

Since the same marketing principle applies across a wide variety of industries, the task of any company researching its markets with an eye toward increasing its presence and market share revolves around getting to know who the leaders and dominant players are. In the process, companies often find that a basic marketing rule holds true: The top 20 percent of the customer population generates 80 percent of the volume.

Find Your Customers' Decision Points

There is nothing revolutionary in this theory of market research. Companies follow this practice all the time. But too many times, they miss the key to doing their research effectively. To successfully understand your customers' business, you must discover where the decision points are in the marketplace. Are the decision points in the head office?

W hen we do our market research, we visit the marketing staff, vice presidents, and presidents of those companies that produce the top 20 percent of our sales. But the people we really want to talk to are out in their top ten stores. They are the operators who are on the front lines—the linchpins in the business. If they say a product or promotion will work, typically it will. If they say it won't work and they won't buy into it, we know we will never get it off the ground, no matter what head office says.

———————

Because the top ten stores generate the business traffic to make or break a product or a promotion aimed at increasing your sales and ultimately your market share, they are the decision points in the marketplace. If you go back to the corporate office of a retailer who has one hundred stores and tell the executives there that nine of their ten top stores want to carry one of your new products, the corporate office will do what works.

Thus, keying into where the real decision-making power lies is critical to your expansion plan, whether you are at the stage of conducting market research, getting a new promotion up and running, or introducing a new product line into the marketplace. Since this is a strategy that works across virtually all industries and all product lines, why don't more companies practice it? Often, going out and talking to the frontline customer creates anxiety. These people don't sit behind desks. They are busy, hard working, and demanding. They have more problems than solutions. When you call on them, you must know your product and their business. It's a very challenging call to make, and it can be intimidating if you are not fully prepared.

For many companies, keeping close to customers by going to the front lines is too demanding. This is especially true of companies that are organized for functional or economic efficiency and think in terms of producing goods rather than satisfying customers. Companies organized this way tend to think in terms of products looking for markets rather than markets looking for products. Stated another way, this simply means that such companies strive to make the market adapt to their production demands rather than working to make their products fit the market's demands.

Make a Commitment to Create Value

Internal expansion depends on creating value for your customers. As the recent rush to philosophies such as "total quality management" and "customer service excellence" indicate, many executives pay lip service to the beginning of the process of creating value—thinking about customer needs.

But they don't carry through, finding it easier to continue to do things as they have always done them. You may improve your marketing, develop new or reformulated products, or open new locations in your current markets, but unless these moves truly represent value for your customers, you won't grow.

A commitment to customer needs that is simply grafted onto a company, rather than generated internally, won't be compatible for long. It might produce a short-lived uptick in market share, but it won't generate long-term growth. The only way senior management, middle management, and all the members of your organization can be dedicated to customer needs is if there is evidence from the top that this kind of activity is the right thing to do for the long-term health of the company. Commitments have to be underscored, in word and deed, starting at the top. At Premdor, for instance, our corporate staff spends the lion's share of its time in front of customers, not behind a desk.

Those executives who make the commitment to carry through on satisfying customer needs, who communicate that commitment throughout their company, and who lead by example, create an environment that encourages growth. Those who don't leave corporate strategy to chance in a rapidly changing business environment.

Improve Your Marketing to Improve Your Market Share

How does keeping close to your customers and knowing customer needs translate into a specific marketing strategy that can increase market share? Look at the following examples.

Example 1. You run a mid-size baking operation and supply a national chain of grocery stores with several specialty products. In order to expand, you want the chain to carry more of your products. Through talking to the managers of the chain's ten most successful stores over the past few years, however, you know that there is going to be more involved than providing them with a good product.

First, you've learned that the business environment for food retailers is changing rapidly. While they wanted to control distribution and inventory in the 1980s, today, their emphasis is on keeping operations lean in order to keep costs down. Thus, they are looking to suppliers to take on a larger role in inventory control and to essentially provide just-in-time delivery of products to their stores. Second, you know that jostling for space on grocery store shelves is fierce business. In order for you to get more space, one of your competitors will have to lose some. That means convincing the grocer that allocating you more space will be more profitable for him.

Clearly, your expansion plan depends on meeting your customer's needs for inventory management, storage, and financial analysis. Over and above the quality of your baked goods and your ability to deliver them, the key to your growth will be your ability to manage information. This might mean coordinating with the chain to use computerized data-gathering equipment to constantly monitor sales and automatically process orders. It will definitely mean getting to know the grocer's business through gathering information on how quickly inventory turns over in the bakery section of his stores and what the profit per foot of shelf space is, for example.

By using this information to help the chain better manage its bakery section and to anticipate the chain's needs, you are changing the way you do business and giving yourself a competitive edge. By staying ahead of the other bakers, you'll wind up with a bigger piece of the pie.

Example 2. Knowing customer needs and being market driven can also help you understand what motivates consumers. Once you know what resonates with people, you can work to develop, improve, or increase awareness of features within your product or service that link into that motivation. Thus you can improve your marketing.

Our standard product is a hollow core wood door. Through staying close to our customers and continually gathering information on the construction and home improvement market, we began to hear that, while the solid look of our doors is popular, a number of consumers associate a heavier door with better quality. It's not difficult to make our doors heavier. By inserting a continuous particle board core, we can give them the same heft as solid wood doors. But is it enough to add weight to our doors, or are consumers really looking for something more?

In the home improvement market today, customers are definitely looking for something more. It is a given that they want to be satisfied that the products they buy will do the necessary job for the best possible price. But more than that, they want to feel good about what they buy. Manufacturers of all kinds of home improvement products, from windows to kitchen cabinets to floor coverings to lighting, have positioned their products to appeal to home owners' yearning for a warm, secure, family-oriented environment. Ads for these types of products consistently show families enjoying an almost nostalgic slice of life inside their cozy homes. The result is that consumers associate the good feelings portrayed with the products advertised.

Premdor's challenge, then, was to determine whether we could link our heavier door into the value system that already exists for other home improvement products. In this case, we found that we could by positioning our door as the Safe 'N Sound door. We had the door tested in outside facilities to establish its fire retardant and sound deadening qualities. As a result, we can market the door as one that improves the quality of home life by making it both safer and quieter. Thus, the consumer who buys a Safe 'N Sound door buys both objective, functional value and subjective, emotional value.

Interestingly, doors are virtually the only home product for which the link into the subjective value system hasn't been made in consumers' minds. This is because the millwork industry simply has never positioned doors as anything other than functional products. And despite the fact that 40 million doors are sold annually in North America, until recently there has been very little brand recognition of door manufacturers at the retail level. Thus, the Safe 'N Sound door is not only an attempt on our part to increase sales through introducing a new product. It's also an attempt to accomplish something much bigger: to develop a selling position and create an image for the company that establishes us as a brand that provides consumers with the values they want.

The Safe 'N Sound door is an example in which improved marketing and new product development overlap. Certainly, this won't happen all the time, but once may be enough.

Example 3. In tough economic times, many companies assume that customers want lower prices. While keeping prices down may be important, it may not be the most important thing to your clients. By keeping close to them and knowing their needs, you may discover that what your customers really want is better service. Thus, improving your marketing may be as basic as improving your customer service. Some companies might find that means assigning specific account managers the responsibility for specific customers. This way, customers feel that someone in your company knows who they are and what they need. Or, it could mean opening more locations in your current market.

Improving customer service could also mean using data more effectively. For example, mail-order clothing businesses maintain extensive computerized records of customers' past purchases. Rather than letting that data sit, the catalogue companies put it to work to establish customer profiles or histories. Thus, when repeat customers call to place orders, the service provided is highly personalized. By accessing the appropriate computer file, the order taker knows the customer's address and the type of payment and shipping arrangements he or she has preferred in the past. The file will also contain information not only on sizes that the customer has ordered in the past, but also colors. Using this data, the order taker can let the customer know if he or she is about to purchase something similar to an item bought previously. This kind of service breeds real customer loyalty. It makes consumers feel as though the company knows them, anticipates their needs, and values their business.

Example 4. For companies doing business in more than one market, serving customers the way they want to be served often means being flexible enough to serve them differently.

In the United States, Premdor's customers are typically large wholesalers, distributors, or retail chains that are capable of purchasing large quantities of doors. Thus, as a rule, we don't maintain a significant finished goods inventory in our U.S. markets. We rely heavily on flexible manufacturing operations together with a fleet of trucks and common carriers to fill our customers' orders.

In Canada, by contrast, we are the manufacturer and distributor, and many of our customers typically place smaller orders with greater frequency. Accordingly, for our Canadian markets, we maintain a finished goods inventory sufficient to enable us to quickly supply our customers' needs. Our manufacturing operations have the capacity to allow us to promptly restock our inventory of finished goods, and our computer system enables us to respond quickly to customer inquiries about the availability of goods, prices, and delivery schedules. It also allows us to control inventory levels without compromising customer service. By maintaining our own fleet of trucks and using outside trucking services as needed, we can adjust shipping schedules to satisfy customer requirements.

Expansion Through Innovation

If knowing customer needs can help you expand through improved marketing, it can also help you expand through innovation. Innovation comes in many different forms. If it's not a new marketing concept, like the Safe 'N Sound door, it could be the creation of:

1. Value-added products; or
2. Good, better, best product lines.

Developing Value-Added Products

Value-added products result from looking at your products through the eyes of your customers and asking:

◆ What does the final user do with my product?

◆ Can I change my product so that consumers will perceive it to be more valuable/more convenient/easier to use?

♦ What combination of price and features represents value to my customers?

U ntil the 1980s, when Premdor sold a door, it was just a door. Then we started to think in terms of what the consumer did with one of our doors once he or she got it home. First, the edge of the door has to be chiseled out for the hinges, the hinges have to be installed, and then the door has to be hung on the frame. If the door did not come with a knob and lock already installed or with predrilled holes for these, the home owner also must drill and chisel openings for this hardware. We then began to wonder what would happen if we did all that work for the consumer and marketed the product as a pre-hung door. This process led to the creation of a value-added product, called the FastFit door, which we market in Canada and sell for about 50 percent more than our standard doors. Through knowing customers' needs, then, we were able to create value for them, which, in turn, creates value for our company.

Extending Product Lines

Good, better, best products have become a popular way to pursue internal growth for manufacturers of all kinds of products, from cars to cookies. Essentially a product line extension, this process involves taking a low-end product, making another version that is a little better, and then making a top-of-the-line version. Starting from the top-of-the-line and working backwards is another variation.

Car makers have been coming out with good, better, best models for years. GM makes Chevrolets and Pontiacs (good), Buicks and Oldsmobiles (better), and Cadillacs (best). Of course, each model also has its own good, better, best entries, and some models even have submodels.

While most products and services can be produced in the good, better, best mode, you will have to have a good understanding of your customers' needs, and of what represents value to them, before rushing into such line extensions. What will the effect be on your existing business and resources if customers end up having little interest in the variations you have created? It usually costs a significant amount to develop a top-of-the-line product, and that product must generate sufficient demand. If GM could sell only a few thousand Cadillacs each year, it would probably abandon the product and focus on higher-volume models. Customers may also reject the added value of the top-line product, figuring they can cope with the middle level entry. Or they may reject the bottom and mid range products in favor of better quality.

The More You Know, the More You Get

Knowledge is key to increasing your market share. You have to know more about your customers than your competitors, and then you have to deliver the goods.

Acquiring the right kind of knowledge is an investment. It has to be part of your expansion planning and budgeting, just as you have to plan and budget for the purchase of machinery or new facilities. Knowledge is a productive asset that is vital to the success of your expansion plan. It should be looked upon in the same way you look at your other productive assets. They need maintaining and upgrading; so does your knowledge base. Your customers' wants and needs are constantly changing, so your knowledge base and the system you use to gather and analyze that knowledge has to adapt to these changes continually.

CHAPTER 4

Going on the Offensive

This chapter discusses expanding beyond your current domestic markets in three ways:

1. Entering new regional markets.

2. Franchising.

3. Building relationships and forming strategic alliances.

Expanding into New Domestic Markets

As discussed in Chapter 3, mounting a solid defense to protect and build your company's position in current domestic markets is the foundation of an effective growth strategy. But on its own it's not enough. What is vital to long-term success, especially for manufacturers, is a strong offense. Going on the offensive means forging into new markets. And, domestically, there are several ways you can go. You can break new ground on your own or you can do it through some form of partnership, for example, through franchising or strategic alliances.

You also can penetrate new domestic markets by acquiring or merging with a company that is located in, or has operations in, a different geographic region. This strategy is discussed in Chapter 5. One of the main differences between growth as described in this chapter and growth through mergers and acquisitions is that the former tends to be a slower, more gradual process, while the latter may transform your company overnight.

And you can go on the offensive by exporting. Because this type of expansion involves accessing foreign rather than domestic markets and comes with its own set of financial and logistical considerations, it is covered separately in Chapters 6 through 8.

The objective of expanding into new markets is to build your company's critical mass so that it will benefit from economies of scale globally, rather than just locally or nationally. Entering new markets is also a means of protecting your position in your current markets. That is because it enables you to learn more about competitors, reduces your vulnerability to the ups and downs of one market or region, potentially allows you to identify new and cheaper sources of raw materials, and can help you become a more efficient—and competitive—producer.

There's No Place Like Home
(and Home Is Not Like Any Place Else)

Many companies make a dangerous assumption when they enter new domestic markets, and that assumption sows the seeds of their failure almost before they begin their expansion. The assumption is that expanding at home is easier than expanding abroad because at home there are no cultural differences—we all live in the same country, speak the same language, use the same currency, buy similar goods, and do business the same way. Wrong. Travel from New York to Los Angeles. Travel from Minneapolis to Dallas. Travel from Montreal to Calgary. It is instantly clear that more than distance separates these cities and their populations. Cultural

---

Figure 4-1. **How to fail in new domestic markets.**

♦ Take it for granted that other domestic markets are the same as your current domestic market.

♦ Presume that because you are successful in your current domestic market you will automatically be successful in other domestic markets.

♦ Fail to do sufficient research on pricing, distribution, and competition in new domestic markets.

♦ Assume that managers and sales representatives can easily be transferred from one domestic market to another.

♦ Assume that advertising and promotional materials that work in one market will work in another.

or regional differences exist across almost all domestic markets. They are not just characteristic of foreign markets. Companies that, either through naivete or ignorance, fail to recognize domestic cultural differences run the risk of failing even when trying to expand in their own backyards. While some companies may offer products or services that can transcend these differences, many do not. This lesson was learned in the 1980s. Overnight success, and easy access to financing, led a number of companies to believe that what worked once in one market would work again, according to exactly the same formula, in many markets. Thus, they bulldozed into new domestic markets with attitudes such as those outlined in Figure 4-1 and didn't survive to tell the tale.

Think Nationally, Act Regionally

Because almost any new domestic market you enter will be different from your current domestic market, the most important thing you can do to ensure success is to develop strong regional management. Very few products or services can be sold in exactly the same way in two different regional markets—even fast-food chains will vary their menus to suit different regions. Thus, you need people on your team who are close to the local market, have experience in it, and understand its customers. They should know the workings of the regional market including the quality standards, methods of distribution, and the competition. And they must be given the power to make decisions locally and run their divisions according to local demands. Obviously, however, controls must be put in place.

Where do you find good regional managers? You may find them working up or down the regional distribution chain for your products. For example, they currently might be employed by one of your regional suppliers or customers. Or they might be working for a competitor in your target market. In such cases, you could consider luring them away.

A s Premdor has expanded throughout Canada, the United States, and Europe, our philosophy has always been to operate on a highly decentralized, regional basis. In Quebec, for example, all our managers are French Canadian, and all have substantial experience in the door business in that region. The logic, and results, of building strong local management are so clear to us that we have never transferred managers from, say, eastern Canada to western Canada or from Canada to the United States. Our own corporate head office in Toronto is a good example of the extent to which the company is decentralized. Our entire staff, including support staff, is just a dozen people.

We have found that even as we become a large company, it is still best to be able to deal with our customers as a regional player. By operating regionally, we can keep our finger on the pulse of our markets, keep abreast of local customer needs, and serve customers the way they want to be served.

———————

If you cannot find a good regional manager in your target market, you will have to parachute in a manager. If this is the case, don't make the mistake of sending someone who either is not ready for the job or is not committed to it. Entrusting a major expansion to a junior manager or to a manager who is not motivated to give his or her best effort is a recipe for disaster.

Develop a Marketing Focus

While it may seem self-evident, there are two salient factors that will determine which new domestic markets you target for expansion:

1. Your corporate objectives.

2. Your knowledge of your industry.

If one of your objectives is to become the dominant player in your region, then the most logical domestic markets to target may be those that are relatively close by. If your current market is the Atlanta, Georgia, area, why target the U.S. Northeast if you do not already have a strong presence in the rest of the Southeast? Remember, however, that one of the long-term objectives of expanding domestically is to give your company some protection against regional economic cycles—if demand is down in the Southeast, it may still be strong in the Northeast, the Midwest, or the West. Thus, targeting markets in a region or regions that, as far as possible, are subject to different economic swings will give you the edge you seek.

Perhaps your corporate strategy for expansion involves establishing yourself as a niche player in new markets. If this is the case, then you would select target markets based on your knowledge about whether they fit key criteria.

Take the example of a fur coat salesman I know. The fact that he is a fur coat salesman in itself may not seem remarkable—except for the fact that he sells his coats in Tampa, Florida. How do you sell fur coats in Florida? Not on the basis of their warmth. The way you sell them is to tap into the customer's desire to look fashionable and affluent. Thus, potential target markets for furs don't necessarily have to be cold and snowy places. Rather, they must be places with a population base that fits two criteria—consumers are concerned with appearances and they are possessed of sufficient disposable income to afford your product. If the market has a weak anti-fur lobby, that will help, too.

Another objective may be to give your company such wide-ranging national presence that you can outmaneuver competitors. In this case, you would likely target numerous markets across the country.

When Premdor introduced the Safe 'N Sound door, as described in the last chapter, one very important factor in our ability to successfully launch the product and create a brand image for the company is our ability to mount national, or even global, campaigns to strongly position both a particular product and the company. We can help our customers sell to their customers by providing national advertising support for certain Premdor products. At the same time, our strong regional orientation enables managers to remain close enough to their local customers to also provide service, merchandising, and marketing initiatives geared to the local market.

———————

Do Your Homework on Potential New Markets

As discussed in Chapter 1, building a solid knowledge base about your industry is one of the core resources that enables you to expand successfully. It equips you with an overall perspective on where your industry is going, what key economic factors are influencing it, and how your competitors are doing. It also helps you spot opportunities and develop a sense of when the time is right to move into a target market. Thus, investing the time in being well-informed pays dividends as it helps you determine where, why, and when to pursue expansion.

To a great extent, informing yourself about domestic markets involves much the same kind of research and fact-finding effort as informing yourself about foreign markets (see Chapter 7). For example, before you enter any new market, some of the areas you will need to find out about include:

- ◆ The regional customer.

- ◆ Market size.

- ◆ The competition.

- ◆ Product demand.

- ◆ Pricing.

- ◆ Methods of marketing and merchandising.

- ◆ Distribution.

- ◆ Transportation and infrastructure.

- ◆ Packaging and labeling regulations.

- ◆ Environmental regulations.

◆ Labor issues.

◆ Tax issues.

◆ Ability of the market to serve as a marketing hub for other regions.

Your information about some of these issues will stem from your commitment to being knowledgeable about your industry. This includes talking to current suppliers and customers to find out whether they have experience in some of the markets you are targeting. You also should be able to obtain information about both general and technical issues from your professional advisors, particularly if they are part of a firm with offices across the country.

But perhaps one of the best ways to inform yourself about potential markets is to regularly attend trade shows. At Premdor, we dedicate a significant portion of travel time and expense to going to these forums. Why? Trade shows offer an unparalleled opportunity to get an overview of different markets. Not only do you see who your potential customers are at trade shows, you also see who your competitors are and what products they are selling.

Some trade shows you'll attend only to gather information. For example, we generally would not consider exhibiting at home shows that appeal directly to the public. But we certainly attend many of them. This is where we see what consumers are looking at and what trends might be developing. We go to see what products, including doors, are on the market. We go to see how the building industry is responding to the home renovation market. We go to see how the building industry is marketing and merchandising its products. We go to talk to our customers' customers.

And, of course, whether you are exhibiting or not, trade shows are used to make contacts with potential distributors, potential customers, and people in the general industry—anyone who can help you sell in your target market.

While doing the trade show circuit and undertaking research and fact-finding on target markets will help you narrow down your options, nothing beats going to the source. Distributing promotional material to and talking up contacts you've met at trade shows or elsewhere isn't enough. If people in new markets are going to buy from you, they want to see you and your product, and they want to do so regularly. Your mission is to sell not only your product, but also the company behind the product. You must convince new buyers that you can deliver service. If they are going to stop buying from a local supplier, they want to be sure that you can give them the service they need when they make the switch. You also have to convince new customers that the product you make is as good as the product they already buy. And you have to have a lot of product knowledge under your belt. You not only have to be able to describe your own product and its benefits, but you also have to be able to draw comparisons to the products your potential customers now purchase.

Expanding Through Franchising

In both the United States and Canada, record numbers of companies are now distributing their goods and services through franchising, and many observers expect franchising activity to continue to be hot throughout much of the 1990s. After all, given today's tight-fisted bankers and business's general aversion to debt, the appeal of financing growth through offering franchises is clear.

Franchising is essentially a way to expand by using other people's money. As a franchisor, you grant franchisees the right to market your product or service in an exclusive territory, usually in exchange for an initial "buy-in" fee plus various regular payments such as royalties on sales or profits, fees for leasing premises and/or equipment, advertising fees, and fees for purchase of inventory or supplies.

Interestingly, franchises are built on the premise of superseding regional differences—no matter where you travel across the country, when you go to a franchise operation you know exactly what to expect in terms of quality, pricing, and service. Uniformity and predictability are paramount.

There is very little that can't be franchised. From every type of food outlet imaginable to any type of retail outlet, to beverage bottling operations, to hotels and motels, fitness clubs, video rental operations, travel agencies, car dealerships, gas stations, automotive part and repair centers, check-cashing services, print shops, hair salons, business products services, package delivery services, nutrition and diet centers, temporary help companies, recycling systems, human resource and management development services—the list goes on. Thus, for almost any business that is short on capital but long on a good concept, becoming a franchisor opens the door to growth. For franchisees, many of whom are out-of-work managers with money from severance packages in their pockets, the opportunity to participate in a large company with national advertising and built-in brand recognition and, at the same time, to become an owner-operator is equally attractive.

Advantages of Expanding Through Franchising

Expanding through franchising can benefit your business in three key areas:

1. Financing.

2. Management.

3. Timing.

Financing.   Properly planned and managed, franchising can provide the financing to expand on a huge scale. In addition to delivering an up-front infusion of capital, franchising also provides the franchisor with future income through regular royalty payments and other fees as previously discussed.

Management.   Companies that expand through opening numerous outlets in their current or new markets often face the problem of managing all those locations. For example, if you run a chain of fast-food restaurants with 200 locations, how do you manage all 200 locations? Do 200 separate managers report to head office? If, instead, you franchise those locations, the franchisee becomes the owner-manager. As the franchisor, you can develop regional managers to assist your franchisees while you also provide them with support services. But you do not have to become involved in managing literally each and every location. Thus, you have the advantages of expanding through opening many locations, but not the potential headaches of overseeing them all.

Timing.   Another advantage of franchising is that it allows relatively quick growth—and profitability. If you have determined that the time is right and the market is ripe for your product or service, then establishing a strong presence before your competitors have a chance to imitate you or capture market share is critical.

However, as has been stated earlier, growing too fast can put you under faster than growing too slowly. If you are overly anxious to sign up franchisees and have not given much consideration to the type of person you want to attract to your business, then you could be headed for problems. Thus, you always have to weigh the benefits of opening more locations against the possibility of having them fail if franchisees are not suited to run the business or if your projections are too optimistic. You also must ensure that you don't make the mistake of oversaturating your markets, for example, by selling new franchises within territories in which you already have a presence. If you are not making money with the locations you currently have, opening more likely won't help. You may receive numerous applications for your franchises, but unless you control the process, you will lose control of your business.

Disadvantages of Expanding Through Franchising

For all its benefits, franchising has a checkered track record. It has been incredibly successful for some companies and utterly disastrous for others. Tales of franchisees suing franchisors and franchisors locking franchisees out of their premises hit the newspapers with some regularity. Such cases have led to the introduction of legislation to regulate the franchise industry in parts of the United States and Canada. Such legislation requires franchisors (at costs that can run from several thousand dollars to tens of thousands of dollars) to file documents containing information on the financial history of the company, the owners and principals of the company, the fee structure, and details about the franchise agreement and any restrictions imposed by it.

Generally, the failure of a franchise rests squarely on the shoulders of the franchisor who either:

1. Fails to deliver value to franchisees, or

2. Loses control.

Obviously, there is more to being a successful franchisor than sitting back and collecting royalties. As a franchisor, you have an ongoing responsibility to your franchisees and to their customers.

Deliver value to your franchisees.   This means providing franchisees with exactly what you promise. This begins with painting a realistic picture of what franchisees can expect from the business they are buying into. The most common reasons for business failure are lack of capitalization and lack of know-how. Thus, it is important to show potential franchisees how you will help them avoid these pitfalls.

As the franchisor, you have the experience to help franchisees realistically estimate what their start-up costs will be, when they can expect to turn a profit—or whether, in fact, they may experience losses in the first year or few years of operation, which is plausible for many businesses—and what they can reasonably expect sales levels to be. Presenting an overly optimistic picture in hopes of selling franchises is a sure way to subvert your expansion plan from the outset. If you don't set realistic requirements for the amount of equity potential franchisees must have before buying in, and thus allow them to buy in with too heavy a debt load, future financial problems will likely be laid at your doorstep whether they deserve to be there or not. Similarly, if franchisees are frustrated by lower-than-expected revenues or are not convinced that they are benefiting from the clout of the franchise group when it comes to purchasing equipment or supplies, they will feel that they have not received value for their buy-in fee, royalties, and other payments.

Some franchisees may have stars in their eyes no matter what projections you present to them. Thus, it is critical that you take the time to carefully screen candidates to assess their personal and financial suitability before accepting their application. Once you have a number of established franchises, you should be prepared to provide the names of the owner-operators to potential franchisees so that they can get a feeling for the business from someone who has been through the process.

Delivering know-how to your franchisees is part and parcel of delivering value. You must be prepared not only to train franchisees to produce your product or deliver your service, but also to run the business and provide them with ongoing support. McDonald's "Hamburger University" is probably the best-known training program for franchisees. Through the course, franchisees learn how to maintain the standards of production and customer service that give McDonald's its image of dependability and quality. In Canada, the Toronto-based company, Second Cup Ltd., the country's largest specialty coffee retailer, puts its franchisees through an intensive training course at "Coffee College" where they learn not only everything there is to know about coffee—where and how beans grow, how to distinguish between types of beans, how beans are roasted and, of course, the best way to brew—but also about how to build and promote customer loyalty, how to hire employees, how to manage cash on a day-to-day basis, and how to keep books, among other things. The theory behind these training courses is that by helping franchisees be better retailers, the franchisors are helping themselves.

As a rule, delivering value to your franchisees also includes:

♦ Developing a network of regional sales managers.

♦ Establishing systems for monitoring and reporting.

♦ Keeping franchisees up to date on the latest technologies and research and development, and giving ongoing training seminars or courses.

♦ Offering assistance with store design.

♦ Providing advertising and marketing support.

♦ Helping franchisees with accounting services and tax advice.

Don't lose control of your business.   Maintaining control over your franchised business and over the quality of the products or service your franchisees deliver begins with your franchise agreement. If the conditions and criteria set out in the agreement do not adequately define how the business is to be run, and on what terms, disputes are likely to arise. Once you grant a franchise, the owner-operator will be running his or her own business. When that business is on its feet, the franchisee will likely want to be as independent from the head office as possible. Unless the obligations of both the franchisor and franchisee are clearly spelled out in the franchise agreement, you will have no control over your franchise operations. Some of the many issues your franchise agreement should address are:

♦ Royalty rates and other fee structures.

♦ Conditions of leasing property and/or equipment.

♦ Supplies and/or inventory franchisees must purchase from you and at what prices.

♦ Pricing structure for products or services sold to consumers by the franchisee and restrictions on pricing policies.

♦ Quality control inspections and how they will be carried out.

♦ Conditions under which the franchisee may purchase a second outlet.

♦ The length of the term of the agreement.

♦ Conditions for termination or transferring the agreement.

♦ Conditions for renewing the agreement.

Maintaining control is also inextricably linked to delivering value. As long as the franchisee feels he or she receives value from the agreement and benefits from following the system as defined by head office, the franchise will work extremely well. As soon as the value and benefits are perceived to fall short of the franchisor's promises, there will be trouble. Thus, many of the elements necessary to deliver value are also necessary to maintain control—conducting thorough screening of applicants to satisfy yourself that they will commit themselves to the company and follow its dictates; presenting realistic financial projections; providing ongoing, up-to-date training; and establishing reliable management support.

Expanding Through Alliances

One relatively quick way to mount an effective offense is to build relationships or work closely with one or two suppliers or customers or complementary producers in a strategic alliance. Such linkups can be forged between domestic companies or they can be cross-border marriages of convenience. Indeed, for Canadian companies, building a relationship with a U.S. partner may not only be one of the best ways to penetrate U.S. markets, it may be necessary for survival. The three-way North American Free Trade Agreement (NAFTA), among the United States, Canada, and Mexico, means that "borderless companies" are bound to multiply. To compete, Canadian companies, especially in certain sectors such as high tech, need a strong offense, and that's what a partnership with a U.S. company can provide. Cross-border alliances offer instant access to foreign markets, are less expensive than setting up your own shop in a new market, and eliminate the need for transferring or hiring management and staff for the new operation. If the alliance is formed with a company that is a particularly experienced and aggressive marketer in a big, mature, or difficult market, the advantages are clear.

A New Approach for the Nineties

Just as the current shift away from debt financing marks a radical change in thinking from the 1980s, so today's growing move toward building relationships is the antithesis of last decade's style of doing business. In the mid- to late-1980s in the United States and Canada, conditions were so good, and demand for products and services was so strong, business forgot what it was like to have to work to sell something. The focus instead was on buying, usually from lots of different suppliers. By playing the field,

---

Figure 4-2. Comparison of eighties and nineties mindsets.

Eighties	Nineties
◆ Concentrate on buying.	◆ Concentrate on selling and buying.
◆ Play suppliers off against each other to get best price.	◆ Cooperate with suppliers to get best quality, service, and price.
◆ Use a multitude of suppliers.	◆ Form strategic alliances with selected suppliers.
◆ Expand any way possible to access new markets.	◆ Stick to what you do best and build relationships up and down the line to access new markets.

businesses could play suppliers off against each other to obtain the best price or terms for purchasing materials or services.

Now that demand has cooled down, the focus is back to selling. As a result, people want to form alliances. It's all part and parcel of business strategy in the 1990s—getting more focused and concentrating on doing what you do best. As Figure 4-2 shows, the new approach requires a fairly dramatic shift in thinking.

The Advantages of Alliances

Strategic alliances can work in several ways. You can have a strategic alliance with a supplier, with a customer, or with the manufacturer of a product that complements your own.

An alliance doesn't have to be exclusive. But to be effective, it has to go beyond the normal relationship you have with your supplier or customer. Building relationships means laying down the 1980s cost-cutting swords and, instead, identifying common objectives and determining how you can work together to accomplish them so that you both can grow.

Common objectives that you could work toward with a supplier or customer might include:

♦ Increasing sales in an existing market.

♦ Accessing a new market.

♦ Increasing sales of an existing product or product line.

♦ Developing and/or marketing a new product or product line.

♦ Improving quality or service.

♦ Maintaining a price advantage.

♦ Locking in a source of supply.

You can build a relationship with another company to achieve a fairly narrow, specific goal. Or, you can use your partnership to achieve broader aims. For example, a large company that specializes in new product design and manufacturing might benefit from an alliance that improved its distribution network. It could then concentrate on what it does best, while the distributor got the finished goods to market. Or, a smaller company in need of hard-to-get capital could ally with a global company in order to continue developing its innovative products.

For the purposes of this discussion, the focus is on how building relationships with suppliers and/or customers can help you grow with control. Taking advantage of the synergies created by such a partnership is essentially a way of expanding without going through the formal process of vertical integration via acquisition or merger. It gives you the advantages of being in two businesses at once without having to invest in two businesses. You can conserve a considerable amount of capital by forming a relationship with a supplier so that you don't have to get into the supplier's business yourself. You can then focus on your business, and the supplier can focus on his or hers. By each sticking to your knitting but also cooperating, you should both achieve better results. If you find a cross-border or international partner, a strategic alliance can also be a means of breaking into foreign markets without the heavy capital commitment required of an exporting venture.

Whether cross-country or cross-border, alliances also can increase your awareness of what competitors are doing, expose you to new ways of doing things, help you improve quality by encouraging you to be tougher on your product and your company, and help you increase your knowledge of your industry.

Some companies worry that tying themselves too closely to a few suppliers, for example, will make them vulnerable. But the types of relationships discussed here are relatively fluid and are not bound by contracts or set in stone. They are based on the two parties sitting down at the table and agreeing to work together. If the arrangement isn't working, it is quickly apparent and you can end it. If it is working, it will continue as long as it produces results.

Premdor's customers are wholesale and retail home supply centers. We don't want to go into our customers' business, but we do want them to expand and increase sales of our products. So we work to help them achieve that end. For example, we don't just ship them our products and leave it at that. We supply our customers with merchandising and marketing programs for our products, and we work with them to develop new products. We also run clinics for their sales staff to show them how a particular product is built, how it works, and what its advantages are. The better they understand a product, the better the job they can do selling it and the more they can sell. Thus, building relationships helps us both grow through increased sales. At the same time, we stay in the business we're in. Our customers stay in the business they are in. But by working together, we both benefit.

Types of Strategic Alliances

As is evident, there are many different reasons for forming and building relationships depending on your objectives and your expansion plan. What follows are just a few possible types of relationships.

The "quality control" relationship.   Businesses today are concerned about how often inventory turns over—thus the advent of just-in-time inventory and just-in-sequence inventory systems. Such systems became particularly important in the North American auto industry in the 1980s. But in the 1980s, auto manufacturers were also dealing with as many as 2,000 suppliers, since playing the field allowed them to beat the suppliers down for price. While they may have won the price war, they often lost the battles on quality and service from suppliers. After all, when you are dealing with 2,000 suppliers, how do you manage your flow of materials? Many auto makers now have begun to form relationships with suppliers, in some cases winnowing the number down from 2,000 to 200. Why? Working with fewer suppliers means control of quality and service.

The "common front" relationship.   Let's say you make just one product—row boats. You know of a number of potential customers to whom you could sell your boats. But it would be much easier to make the sales if you could approach them not only with your boats, but also with oars. You could always expand by buying a company that makes oars and marketing the row boats and oars together. Or, you could form an alliance with an oar maker who has the same problem going to potential customers because he doesn't make row boats.

The "two-way street" relationship.   Premdor built this type of relationship with another door manufacturer in the United States. They make a product that, at one point, we did not make—exterior solid wood doors— and we make a product that they don't make—hollow core flush doors. Through our alliance, we have helped each other expand. We sell their product in Canada and they sell ours in the United States, and we both increase sales. Thus, our relationship is a two-way street. It can be more difficult to find a partner to link up with in this way, but if you do, the result is usually a very powerful alliance.

The "mutual marketing" relationship.   For most businesses, the decision to deal with a particular supplier is based largely on price. But if you look further than price, you may see how a relationship can benefit both of you. Say your product has a certain level of awareness among consumers, and you are willing to put a specified amount of money toward marketing and merchandising the product. What if you could build a relationship with a supplier who knows that every time you sell your product you are using his material? Why not form an alliance with him through which he contributes to the marketing and merchandising of your product and, indirectly, his material? By taking your resources and adding his resources, you will be getting a much bigger bang for your marketing buck.

The "piggy-back export" relationship.   If you are developing an export strategy, forming an alliance with one of your major suppliers could help you both. If you sell your product abroad, you are selling your supplier's product abroad. If your sales increase sales, his sales to you increase. If you do better, he does better. On this basis, your supplier could be willing to give you extended terms—for instance, providing inventory on a consignment basis. Or maybe the two of you could establish a cost-sharing relationship. Perhaps your supplier will sell you materials at a lower initial cost in order to give you an edge in opening up the overseas market. Or maybe you could share development costs or marketing and merchandising costs. It's good for the supplier and it's good for you.

The Bottom Line Is Profitability

No matter what form your alliance takes, the emphasis should always be on the bottom line—are you making more profit?

If your alliance is with a supplier, this may mean that, from time to time, you may not be paying the lowest price for a certain material. But does buying the cheapest material always translate into higher profit? There may be quality or service problems with a cheaper material. Or there may be problems with warranties. In many cases, if you pay more for a dependable material or component, you can charge more for your finished product. What is cost effective in the long term, not the short term, is the priority. For years, Japanese auto manufacturers have used strategic alliances with suppliers of everything from steel to electronic components. The guiding philosophy is: If, together, we build the best car, then we'll all do well in the long run. By working in unison with their suppliers to develop new products and new markets, they not only built a dominant position in the world auto market, they began to define it. Other manufacturers were left to react to the agenda set by the Japanese.

Alliances Call for a Change in Attitude

Building relationships or forming strategic alliances is, more than anything else, a change in attitude. Figure 4-3 shows how the change can be schematized.

Because change is rarely easy, companies often find it a barrier to forming relationships. After all, relationships with suppliers traditionally have been built on a day-by-day or month-by-month basis. Working for the long term with suppliers demands a different attitude, and sharing information changes the way of negotiating.

Some people view alliances with suspicion or wariness. They believe that working closely with a particular customer or supplier may create the

---

Figure 4-3.   **Old attitudes are giving way to new.**

combative	→	cooperative
protect information	→	share information
loner mentality	→	teamwork approach

perception of an exclusive relationship. But how important is that perception in the long run? And what is more important—that perception or the bottom line? What you need to think about is how building relationships will benefit you. If a close association gets you where you want to be, what is the difference if you do it with two suppliers or two hundred? If you can achieve increased market share, growth, and greater profitability by dealing with fewer people and building relationships, why not?

Don't Just Make Your Piece of the Pie Bigger— Make the Pie Bigger

Improved marketing, adding value to your products, extending your product lines, entering new markets, and forming alliances are all ways of increasing market share. Through them, you work towards getting a bigger piece of the pie. But your internal expansion plan should always have another dimension—trying to make the pie bigger.

The More Takers, the Bigger the Pie

Most products are developed and marketed with a particular class of buyers in mind. If you can tap into another class of buyers, you usually can stimulate additional demand for a product.

═══════════

M ost of Premdor's competitors concentrate on selling doors for use in new home construction. Yet, in many markets around the world, new housing is locked into a cyclical, nongrowth pattern because of demographic factors influencing demand. While we are a major player in selling doors to the new home construction industry, we recognize that this market has its limitations. Thus, in order to become bigger, we have had to find ways to create demand for our products among other buyers in other markets. One of those is the home improvement market.

Like all of us, preexisting homes are aging. Rather than "trading up" to a more expensive place to live, many people look to renovation and remodeling as the most economical way to update and improve the quality of their homes. In the past, however, door replacement has not been a renovation priority for North American home owners. By working to convince home owners to replace their old, hardboard slab or stained doors with one of the company's new moulded door designs, Premdor can make the door market pie bigger. Thus, much of our advertising and merchandising, including point-of-sale displays and in-store decorating seminars, is geared toward showing customers how important new doors can be to their remodeling projects.

The marketing of cellular telephones is another example of a product tapping into new markets. Car phones originally were sold as a business tool for executives and traveling sales representatives. Now, however, car phones are successfully promoted to all drivers both as a convenience and a safety device in case of an emergency or a breakdown.

Two Is Better Than One

Typically, most products are initially marketed with the idea of placing one in every home. Once most homes have one, demand drops off and the marketplace becomes very stable as worn out units are replaced by new ones. However, if you can convince buyers that their lives will improve dramatically if they have two of your product, demand will pick up.

A classic example of making the pie bigger in this fashion comes, once again, from the auto industry. It created a demand for second cars by making compacts that were both fuel efficient and affordable. In so doing, it became easy for families to justify having a second car. A compact costs a lot less than the big family car and is perfectly suited for errands around town or shuttling commuters to and from work or transit connections to work. Meanwhile, the bigger family car is still there for family outings.

The television manufacturing industry also exploited this opportunity by marketing different size televisions and showing several being used by different members of the family. We are now to the point where one-television households are a rarity in North America.

A Bigger Pie Is a Better Pie

The point of making the pie bigger is obviously to increase sales and grow. As the previous examples suggest, the recipe for this kind of growth generally calls for innovative marketing and merchandising. There are advantages to pursuing this growth strategy:

1. If you are the first to market to a new segment of customers, you don't have to take existing market share away from your competitors.

2. You are not in the position of adding extra capacity that cannot be sold profitably.

3. Your exposure to cyclical ups and downs is reduced by diversifying your markets. If demand for new homes is weak, demand for renovation products may be up or at least stable. If demand for large family cars is stalled, demand for economical compacts may be speeding up.

4. You may be able to become a lower-cost producer. If you have excess plant capacity, adding volume may mean that your unit costs decline. If you are sending more of your product into the marketplace, you may be able to take greater advantage of distribution channels.

Of course, your success will attract the attention of your competitors who also will come after a bigger piece of the now-bigger pie. However, by being there first you have an advantage and, if you have planned properly, you can use this advantage to be more competitive.

CHAPTER 5

Expanding Through Acquisitions and Mergers

In this chapter, growth via acquisitions and mergers is reexamined for the 1990s, with emphasis on:

♦ What an acquisition or merger can, and can't, do for your company.

♦ Why so many corporate marriages fall apart.

♦ What commitments this type of growth requires.

♦ How to maintain control of the process.

Advice on Acquisitions and Mergers from the Horse's Mouth

Lots of good books on acquisitions and mergers have already been written. So how can the same topic really be given justice here in only one chapter? The answer is that almost all those other books, good and useful as they may be, were written by outsiders looking in—accountants, lawyers, university professors, consultants. Few, if any, were written by insiders—a company president, CEO, CFO, or other corporate officers who have actually sat at the negotiating table and then, after closing the acquisition or merger deal, managed the process of integrating the companies involved. Other books can take you through the accounting, legal, and tax implications of an acquisition or merger. This chapter will take you through the process, business to business.

The Benefits of Tying the Corporate Knot

Acquisitions and mergers got a bad reputation in the 1980s. Companies bought or merged with other companies in industries they knew nothing about—and went into massive debt in the process. Profitable, healthy target companies often became casualties as their resources were used to prop up other, ailing companies in the acquisitor's stable. Misguided expansion agendas seemed to be the order of the decade.

Yet, many acquisitions and mergers in the 1980s did make sense. Numerous computer companies, for example, acquired or merged with each other, but always stayed within their industry. And they expanded from positions of financial and management strength. The common sense that typified their growth strategies means that most are still prospering in the 1990s.

Properly planned and executed, corporate marriages can be made in heaven. That's because the synergy they create, the total effect of the union, is greater than the sum of the individual parts. In successful acquisitions and mergers, one plus one makes three, not two.

Consider these four key benefits of growing through tying the corporate knot.

1. *Efficiency gains.* Putting two companies together can result in economies of scale in production and rationalization of production, with specific plants specializing in the manufacture of specific items. A corporate marriage also can result in reduced financing costs as two companies together may not require the same level of inventory that they would individually. And the union may mean that redundant assets can be sold.

2. *Savings and profitability.* Even if sales volumes for the new entity are only equal to the combined sales of the two original companies, the company still will enjoy higher profitability because of the savings realized from efficiency gains. Thus, one plus one actually makes three.

3. *Long-term viability.* Even more important than the short-term boost to profits are the ongoing advantages of expanding through acquisition or merger. As we've seen, for many companies today, the key to survival and success rests in the ability to sustain a concerted effort to enter new markets in North America and abroad. Through acquisitions and mergers, companies can realize synergies in sales, marketing, distribution, geographic location,

purchasing power, production, and technology that will allow them to push ahead. And they can combine research and development activities to facilitate the development of new products and new technology.

4. *Strength and vitality.* Corporate unions often breed new strength by adding depth to the management team. Such strength usually provides an edge over the competition. The advantages of a marriage between an aggressive, entrepreneurial newcomer and a seasoned veteran, for example, can significantly enhance chances for success in fast-changing global markets.

Your Future May Depend on It

Any of these benefits seems ample justification for tying the corporate knot. But there is another reason to acquire or merge with a partner, and it's a reason that is often overlooked. Acquisitions and mergers are often pursued because at least one of the partners forecasts that it won't do as well in the future as it has done in the past.

At the end of 1988, before Premdor merged with Century Wood Door Limited, both companies had healthy sales and market share and both were in good financial shape. But when we looked ahead, what was in store? Globalization of trade was becoming the order of the day. At the same time, North American housing construction was at the brink of a sharp, three-year contraction. Thus, in our situation, it seemed that the best way to survive into the 1990s and beyond was to build a bigger company with the critical mass, efficiency, and clout that would enable us to compete not only in North America, but also around the world.

In many ways, the big economic picture hasn't changed much since the mid- to late-1980s. Because of global competition, the portrait of many North American companies looks like this:

- ♦ They face more competition as trade barriers come off.
- ♦ They face shrinking markets.
- ♦ Their cost structures are inefficient or, even if they were efficient during the 1980s, increased competition means those same cost structures won't work as well in the 1990s.
- ♦ They are terrified that they will lose, or are losing, their ability to compete.

Not a pretty picture. To the company that sees the economic writing on the wall, there is an obvious need to improve its competitive position for the long term. Thus, for many, bigger is justifiably better.

And, for many, the sooner they grow bigger, the better. Expansion through acquisition or merger, as opposed to slow but steady internal growth, has the very real advantage of giving a company an instant hit. One day the company is a certain size; the next day it may have doubled, thus immediately enjoying more buying clout, economies of scale, increased revenues, and all the other advantages held by big players.

In September 1991, when Premdor bought three U.S. companies in a major acquisition, we instantly increased our revenues by $120 million. Overnight, we were in two new product lines—steel doors and architectural doors. This type of growth is obviously quite different from beginning with a start-up situation in new markets and nurturing growth. Because our objective is to become a stronger, more competitive, global company, it makes more sense for us to acquire the management, people, customers, machinery, products, and new markets we need rather than to build these resources up slowly.

What Can Go Wrong?

For all the advantages of acquisitions and mergers, however, the fact is that like many marriages, they often don't work out. The three main reasons that corporate marriages break down are:

1. *A shotgun wedding.* One or both parties fail to get to know each other well enough, particularly financially, before tying the knot.

2. *Poor planning and/or poor communications.* If the goals and objectives of the new, expanded company are not clear or are not clearly communicated to managers and employees, some never will buy in.

3. *Culture clash.* While the deal may make perfect sense on paper—the numbers work, the savings are there, and the synergies to be created would translate into profit—in practice, the partners just can't live together.

It's also important to note that while some acquisitions and mergers may not fail, neither may they succeed at actually making a business grow significantly. For example, suppose your company integrates vertically and buys one of its suppliers. You won't necessarily grow if your company accounts for all of the sales of the new company. Or, if you acquire or merge with another company in your existing market, room for growth may be limited. There may be problems of duplication. Can you maintain a market share equal to, or larger than, the sum of the market share of the two individual companies? What will customer reaction be? Without proper planning, you may find that you have gone through a lot of work only to have kept half the existing business you bought and improved your market share just marginally. When a company expands by acquisition or merger into a new market, by contrast, problems of duplication are not an issue—it wants the sales force, the management, and the presence in the new market because it currently doesn't have them.

Planning the Process

It is clear that, like civil marriages, corporate marriages demand a lot of work in order to succeed. And the lion's share of that work is in the planning. That planning begins with defining what you want to accomplish through expansion since this will help you identify appropriate acquisition or merger candidates. For example:

♦ If your strategic plan is to expand into new markets, then obviously you'll look farther than your own backyard for a target.

♦ If your goal is to become the low-cost producer and largest distributor in your industry, you will think about joining ranks with a competitor.

♦ If your company has one major piece of the profit puzzle, such as research and development capabilities, you will look for a partner with the potential to complete the picture, one with superior production and marketing capabilities.

B ecause Premdor is a manufacturer whose strategic plan is to become a global company, it makes sense for us to grow through acquisition. One of the most important reasons is that acquisitions give us experienced regional management in geographic areas that are key to our growth. Through acquisition of a company in 1991, for example, we added management strength in two areas—the U.S. midwest and central regions—where previously we were weak. One year later, we continued to build strength in areas needed to complete our national coverage by buying a company in California. These acquisitions, then, not only enabled us to consolidate our North American presence, they also gave us access to strong managers in the new areas.

Bear in mind that it is much easier to control and succeed at an acquisition if the company you buy is in your own industry. If you are a door manufacturer who acquires a brick manufacturer, you will be dealing with a new customer base, new suppliers, and new distributors. Performing a satisfactory review of the target company will also be more difficult because your learning curve for the new industry will be high.

You also should be cautious about buying small, entrepreneurial companies, especially if the owner-manager stays on. Trying to live together can be like trying to put a saddle on a horse to break the horse. In many instances, you're better off without the disruption, despite the entrepreneur's talent and track record.

While defining what you want in a partner and what you want from your corporate marriage helps you develop a focus, it is also important to concentrate on planning for the eventual impact that an acquisition or merger will have on your management, employees, customers, suppliers, banking, and financing. This type of planning calls for commitment—and lots of it. As president or CEO, one of your major commitments will be that of time. In fact, preparation for an acquisition or merger can become a full-time job in itself. Since many corporate marriages take at least six months to complete, you must be willing to delegate day-to-day management of your business to your managers and understand the added stress that they will be under.

As you embark on pursuing expansion through acquisition or merger, you will find that a corporate marriage, like any marriage, proceeds in four distinct stages:

1. Courtship.

2. Engagement.

3. Tying the knot.

4. Working to make the marriage last.

Courtship

As in personal life, corporate courtship often begins with a phone call. Perhaps, like some companies, you have one or more people on staff whose job is to hunt for and analyze acquisition or merger opportunities, and they have turned up a promising candidate with whom you wish to talk. Or maybe an intermediary such as an investment banker or a "matchmaker" has put you in touch. In any case, if after an initial phone call you agree to meet, talk at the meeting will be general. Neither party will divulge competitively sensitive information, but if the meeting goes well, others will follow.

During the courtship period, you will be conducting a cursory review of the target company. While you both will be making assumptions about each other, you also will be trying to get as much information as possible before taking the next step—signing a letter of intent, or becoming engaged. If you both use the same suppliers and have some of the same customers, it may be useful to talk to them. Ex-employees of the target company are also good sources of information.

Should you have a chance, walk through the target company's facilities and plant. Just looking around can tell you a great deal. Is equipment well-maintained and up-to-date? Are basic safety regulations followed? Does production appear to be well-organized and efficient? If not, poor management is in evidence, and you would likely want to reconsider before going much further with the deal.

If outside parties such as investment bankers or business brokers are involved in a potential acquisition or merger, be sure you know their agenda. They may convincingly reassure you that the economic slump is almost over in the region where you are considering buying a company. But always get lots of corroboration from other sources. And remember that investment bankers or brokers get a commission if the sale goes through.

If, during the courtship period, you decide not to go further, don't feel that you've wasted time. It is in your best interest to look at any opportunity to acquire or merge with a company in your industry. Even if the opportunity is only of passing interest, it is nevertheless an opportunity to learn more about the dynamics of the industry.

A t Premdor, hearing that another door company or a supplier is up for sale is like a call to attention. With four professional accountants and a lawyer as corporate officers, we find that we can size up an opportunity fairly quickly. It might take three to four weeks to analyze the possible purchase from different perspectives and perhaps visit the target company's premises. Whether we proceed further or not, we always feel that we have come out ahead by being curious.

Engagement

If courtship has led you to believe that a corporate marriage could succeed, then it's time to get more serious. When you consent to become "engaged," you both will sign an agreement or letter of intent setting out the terms for the acquisition or merger. These agreements usually are conditional on the due diligence process—a process of in-depth investigation—which will be performed before closing the deal.

Throughout your engagement, your purpose is threefold. You want to:

1. Assess the opportunities (the synergies that would be created) and alternatives (perhaps you should opt for increased specialization or even selling your company).

2. Assure yourself that the marriage would be profitable.

3. Determine whether the two companies can live together as a new entity.

Remember, one of the main reasons mergers fail is that the parties didn't get to know each other well enough.

During this period, it is up to you to ensure that you become completely familiar with the target company, while avoiding revealing any sensitive information about your company. At this point, the involvement of legal and accounting advisors is also essential.

It also will be critical for you to have discussions with key management, sales, and production people not only to get information about operations, but also to get a feel for their attitudes, for the state of labor relations at the company, and for the company's corporate philosophy.

This is also the time to broach the subject of who will head up the new operation. A company can have only one CEO. If there is to be a power struggle, it must be worked out now or it will never be resolved. At the same time, plans must be laid for the CEO who is stepping aside. It may be possible to create a position for this person or perhaps he or she is looking forward to retiring.

Valuing the Company

During the engagement period, you should perform a detailed review of the target company's financial information to get a picture of its financial performance and condition—past, present, and future.

If you are acquiring the target company, you also must set a value on it. While you probably have an idea of the target's asking price, you must determine your own opinion of its value or be able to justify a different asking price. When it comes to setting the purchase price, it is important to draw a distinction between acquisitions made strictly for investment purposes, such as those often made by holding companies, and acquisitions made for strategic purposes. A strategic purchase will have long-term effects on your existing business in terms of the synergies created and the benefits produced. Thus, calculating the strategic value of the purchase is often more important than calculating the value as determined by standard valuation methods.

For example, according to standard valuation techniques, it would be a bad business decision to pay a lot of money for a company that, perhaps due to a recession, is not earning a lot of money. But what if the target company gives you access to a new domestic market that is strategically important to you and sets you up with experienced management and personnel, a plant, and a solid customer list? Combined with the benefits you can bring to the target company—technology, purchasing power, marketing and merchandising support, and complementary product lines—what is its value? An "earnings multiple" formula would indicate that the value of the target company in a period of years when it had no earnings is nil. A "payback" formula might indicate that you should make back the money spent on the acquisition in three years in order for it to be a good deal. But, if the purchase allows you to acquire good regional management, a five-year payback may be perfectly acceptable.

The point is that standard valuation techniques should not be the sole measure for determining the value of an acquisition, especially if you are growing strategically. If you are growing strategically, the value of the target company should be based on the extent to which it helps you achieve overall corporate objectives. For example:

♦ Does the acquisition enable you to increase sales and improve your positioning?

♦ Will you be able to rationalize existing operations by acquiring assets of the target company?

♦ Will you be acquiring good management and personnel?

♦ Are you getting additional product to add to your existing lines, not only in the target company's market but in all of your markets?

♦ Are you obtaining a solid customer base?

♦ Are you purchasing state-of-the-art technology?

Any or all of the above create long-term value for your company. And such future value can be a more important measure of value than, say, historical earnings. While traditional techniques for measuring value should be used as guidelines, placing too much emphasis on them can blind you. This is particularly true if you let your professional advisors dictate what you should buy. When you value a target company, your main concern should not be what someone else is getting, but what you are getting.

Remember, however, that the one issue you always must be concerned with when valuing a company is its balance sheet. You must ensure that the acquisition will not saddle you with a heavy debt load and liabilities that will have a negative impact on your existing business. You also should take care that you do not get yourself into a turnaround situation. The amount of time and attention management must devote to such troubled companies rarely makes these projects worthwhile. There are many reasons that, from time to time, a good company may not be profitable; perhaps it is paying too much for materials or perhaps demand for its products has hit a seasonal low. That is a far cry from a company that has lost substantial amounts of money, is laden with debt, and has weak management. Such companies usually have problems to be addressed at all levels—including the ability of their people, their financing, the quality of their products, the need for investment in machinery and equipment, and the need to turn around a bad reputation among customers and suppliers—and thus should be avoided.

Lessons in Due Diligence

Not enough can be said about the importance of the due diligence process. It takes tremendous time and effort, and there is no substitute for it.

Interestingly, during the merger and acquisition frenzy of the 1980s, some very reputable companies thought that money might be a substitute for due diligence. We found this out in 1991 when we acquired a door manufacturer that had, in turn, been acquired by another company in the mid-eighties. During our due diligence process, we discovered that the target company did not have clear title to some of its real estate and, therefore, had no title insurance for those properties thus making financing the deal difficult. Executives at the company admitted that they hadn't taken the time to check the titles because the acquisition was just one of many they were making at the time.

In our experience, hindsight is 20-20. Whenever a problem has cropped up after an acquisition, we've always been able to look back and see a question we didn't ask or to identify an area that we didn't research well enough. If you cannot perform the due diligence that you want to perform, if your intended balks at the process or your thoroughness, don't hesitate to break off the engagement and walk away from the deal.

To a certain extent, being good at the due diligence process takes experience. A company that has been through it several times—and has learned from its mistakes or oversights—will do a better job at it than a company conducting the procedure for the first time. If you are experienced in due diligence, you and your management team will be able to conduct much of the review on your own.

A team of professionals, including lawyers, accountants, and environmental experts, however, also will be involved in any preacquisition or premerger review. When it comes to this team of professionals, make sure they have experience in mergers and acquisitions. Your lawyer and accountant may be very good at what they do, but if they have never performed due diligence or been through the acquisition or merger process, you will be at a disadvantage. It is worth noting that while you want the very best advisors you can get, you shouldn't hesitate to negotiate fees. There is nothing wrong with trying to minimize costs associated with using the services of bankers, lawyers, and accountants. Finally, remember that while there is no substitute for the input of professionals, there is also no substitute for some lessons learned through experience.

Lesson 1: It's important to look back at a company's financial picture—but you also have to try to look behind the picture.   Through the due diligence process, you will delve into the financial and operational details of the target company. Your financial review will look back at the historical performance of the company. Your goal is to ensure that the financial presentations that have been made to you are correct. Are the payables and debt really what the target company contends they are? Is the target's claim to have earned a profit of $1 million last year valid? Through examination of audited statements, you should be able to satisfy yourself on such matters.

But you also want more than just the facts. If the company made a profit, for example, you want to discover whether there are any unusual reasons for the company's performance. Is the core business throwing off the profit or was there a one-off transaction, such as the sale of assets, that caused a blip in the profit picture? As a rule, your review of balance sheets and income statements should go back five years so that you can get behind the initial numbers and compare performance over a meaningful stretch of time. Sellers, of course, are always reluctant to bare their souls. But the incentive of receiving a good price for their company is usually enough to encourage their cooperation.

An often neglected but essential part of the historical review is developing an understanding of trends affecting the business over the last five years. Have material costs been rising? Have trade agreements affected the market? Again, your goal is to go beyond the numbers contained in the financial statements and determine what has been going on to create those numbers or to skew them. It is also important to look into contingencies (off-balance-sheet potential liabilities). Your decision on whether to close the deal should include investigation of the company's potential to be drawn into lawsuits, cases of product liability, warranty contingencies, cases involving corporate fraud, and so on.

Lesson 2: If it's important to look back, it's crucial to look forward. It's one thing to satisfy yourself that the target company has indeed been financially sound, and hopefully profitable, for the past five years. But what about next year, or the year after? All the time and planning you and your team invest in researching the company's past won't be worth a thing unless you invest equal effort in looking at the future. Consider the following questions:

♦ If the company has performed well, has anything happened that will make it difficult to repeat that performance?

♦ If it performed well in a boom, how will it do in a bust?

♦ Has it lost a major customer?

♦ What are the owners' financial reasons for selling? Do they know something you don't know? Are they forecasting that they won't do as well in the future? Why?

Putting together budgets, cash flow projections, and forecasts, and undertaking sensitivity analyses to examine the company's future performance in certain scenarios will enable you to understand the effect of putting the two companies together.

As part of the planning process, you should consider not only economic factors that may affect the target company but also practical matters. If the company has a lease, you would obviously want to find out what the terms are and when the lease expires. But you would also have to look beyond that. What happens if rents will be going up when it's time to renew the lease? Will you have to shop around locally for new space or perhaps even move the business to another city? When looking forward, you also need to try to develop an idea of what factors could affect the current picture of the target company.

Planning for the future also should include deciding on matters such as how to control receivables, inventories, payables, accounting systems, computer systems, and administrative systems in the new company. You also may have to decide what plants, if any, should be closed and which assets sold.

If you intend to expand through a merger, the financial side of the new ownership will have to be determined. Some issues to be negotiated will include share structure and dividend payments, and banking and loan arrangements.

Lesson 3: Environmental issues are *the* issue of the 1990s.   An environmental audit can make or break a deal, and you won't get to first base at the bank without one. Five years ago, the environmental review process barely existed. Today, hiring the best environmental expert you can get to perform an audit on land and buildings is one of the most important parts of the due diligence process. The reason for this rapid and radical shift in business practice can be explained through a cautionary tale.

Not long ago, in the western United States, there was a company that went bankrupt. When the bank foreclosed on the company, it became owner of the land and building. Soon afterwards, a major environmental problem was discovered on the property. To its dismay, the bank found out that, as current owner of the property, liability and responsibility for the cleanup of environmental contamination rested in its hands even though the previous owner caused the problem. Banks across North America took the lesson to heart very, very quickly—they now will not take land and buildings as security unless the property is certifiably "clean." Indeed, banks are so serious about this issue that a "Twilight Zone" class of properties is now emerging across the United States and Canada—no one owns the properties and no one wants to. Their former owners went bankrupt, the banks refuse to foreclose, and there are no buyers in sight.

In both the United States and Canada, determining liability for environmental problems is like a game of musical chairs. If you own the property when the music stops, you hold the bag for its cleanup. And that bag can be huge—multimillion dollar cleanups are not unheard of.

While calling in the environmental experts should, in theory, give you and your bank a level of comfort about the condition of the property owned by the company you wish to acquire or merge with, bear in mind that there is still a subjective aspect to the environmental audit. The environmental specialists will point out risks and factors to be considered when assessing a property, but they will not express an opinion on the property. It is up to you as the purchaser, or your bank as the lender, to evaluate the risks identified and make the business decision about whether to proceed.

Some of the most basic questions you will have to answer include:

♦ Will environmental problems at the target company endanger your existing business? Will the cost of cleaning up its business destroy the viability of your business? Will getting the target company onside environmentally sap your financial resources?

◆ What is the history of property owned by the target company? Have environmental reviews been conducted in the past? With what results?

◆ What is the target company's "green plan"? That is, how does it currently dispose of hazardous waste? What emergency response strategies are in place in case of a hazardous material spill or other hazardous situation? What monitoring systems does the company have in place?

Because Premdor's expansion has included close to a dozen acquisitions, we have composed our own detailed environmental due diligence checklist. A copy of it is included as Appendix A at the back of the book.

Lesson 4: This is a lesson in chemistry—corporate chemistry. During the due diligence process, people tend to concentrate on objective issues, such as verifying financial statements and assessing the value of real estate and equipment. Subjective issues, such as assessing people and corporate cultures, are passed over with the idea that they aren't important or can be fixed later. They are almost always important and, many times, they cannot be fixed later.

If you expand through acquisition or merger, it's possible that certain people may not be comfortable with the new organization, or that the new organization may not be comfortable with them. Part of your due diligence process is to try to "read" and understand the cultural chemistry of the target company, foresee where problems might arise and, where possible, avert those problems. Thus, it's important to interview senior people at the target company. You want to get a feel for their attitudes toward the proposed corporate marriage and their likelihood of staying on after the deal is closed. This is especially important if you are buying a target company in order to expand into a new geographic area or expand your product line. Ideally, you want to keep the knowledge and experience of those familiar with that market or product within the company. If you know that the owner-manager or owners will be leaving fairly soon after the closing, then it's important to try to assess the abilities of those working directly under them. In addition, you also want to assess management style at the company. A company with a tradition of good management practices is a more attractive acquisition candidate than one without that track record. A partial due diligence checklist for assessing management at the target company might look like that in Figure 5-1.

Don't forget that due diligence on the human resources front is not restricted to management. Your review and planning also need to extend to the rank and file. For example, if the target company's employees are unionized and yours are not, how will you handle the situation?

Lesson 5: It's never too early to work on your vision of the future. Developing a vision for the new, expanded company grows, in part, from your strategic plan and from the kind of cultural review discussed previously. But it also grows from the operational review that is conducted during the due diligence process.

Specifically, through your operational review, you will gather detailed information on, among other things:

Figure 5-1. A partial checklist for assessing management at a target company.

	Yes	No
1. Is the target company so entrepreneurial that things will fall apart if a key person, or people, leave?	☐	☐
2. Are staff working under current managers likely to stay on?	☐	☐
3. If promoted, are current junior managers up to the task of running the operation?	☐	☐
4. If key people do leave, do you have excess talent within your organization who can be parachuted into the new operations?	☐	☐
5. Does management regularly communicate with and hold meetings with staff?	☐	☐
6. Is initiative visibly encouraged and rewarded?	☐	☐
7. Is there a history of promotion from within the company?	☐	☐
8. Does management encourage, and pay for, employees to take professional training or upgrading courses?	☐	☐
9. Are staff encouraged to become involved in professional or industry associations?	☐	☐

- ◆ Industry conditions.
- ◆ Customer needs.
- ◆ Sales and distribution networks.
- ◆ Size, location, and condition of plants and equipment.
- ◆ Number of employees.

From this information, the structure of the new organization has to be created.

Will you create a number of new operational divisions when the acquisition or merger is implemented, or are divisions to be consolidated? If the plan is for new divisions, who will manage them and what will be the chain of reporting and responsibility? The answers to these operational questions stem from your human resources "audit."

When Premdor and Century Wood Door Limited merged in 1989, we immediately implemented a plan to restructure existing operations. The basis of the plan was to reorganize the company into five regional operating divisions, each with a profit center under the direction of a general manager who, in turn, reported directly to the CEO. Sales and production were relocated to the most efficient plants in order to eliminate duplication. The rationalization process lasted into 1990. Some of the steps we took included:

- ◆ Discontinuing operations in several locations across Canada and the United States.
- ◆ Consolidating distribution operations.
- ◆ Selling redundant manufacturing facilities.
- ◆ Restructuring and streamlining certain product lines.

While it's essential to have your short-term strategy mapped out so that the new organization, and its people, have an immediate sense of direction once the corporate marriage takes place, don't forget that you must also create and explain your long-term vision. This vision must clearly set out the new company's goals and objectives over the next five years and must define the kind of business you want to be, the markets you want to be in, your sales and employment targets, and your corporate philosophy. You're only ready to tie the knot when the vision is clear.

Lesson 6: Don't forget to loosen up a little during the due diligence process—and don't forget to listen.   In the midst of the formalities of the due diligence process, doing something impromptu and informal can pay off. By taking the time to talk casually with the principals of the target company, you can learn about things that don't come up in the documentation and may not come up in the formal discussions. A single comment can lead you to an avenue of investigation that you might have otherwise missed—but you have to be a good listener.

We learned this lesson a few years ago, during the process of one of our acquisitions. Our due diligence team members had put in a long day working with several managers at the target company when one of our people suggested, on the spur of the moment, that we all should go out for a casual dinner. While we talked at the restaurant, one of the people from the target company mentioned that the vice president of marketing planned to retire in two years. Because we were new to the area, we had been counting on keeping his expertise in the company. He never told us he was contemplating retirement and, because he was only 55, it never occurred to us that he might be. By finding out in advance, we were able to work out a plan with him to bring in someone else with experience in the market.

There are, of course, many other areas in which you will need to conduct due diligence when you are in the process of expanding through an acquisition or merger. Appendix B at the back of the book contains a summary of Premdor's due diligence checklist.

Why People Fail to Do Effective Due Diligence

One of the main reasons why people fail to do proper or sufficient due diligence is because they go too much by the book. They concentrate on the headings listed in their due diligence manual, look at the things that are easy to look at, and don't think of going any further.

For example, your due diligence manual or checklist might tell you to review trademarks held by the target company. But it's not just a matter of searching the trademark registry to see that trademarks have been properly registered by the company. What the manual doesn't tell you is that there is more to it than that. Suppose that three months earlier the validity of one of the trademarks had been questioned. What you really want to know when you review trademarks is whether there have been any challenges. Trademarks are valued very highly—if one held by the target company has become generic in the market, like Kleenex, how will this affect your plans? Unless you ask the right questions, you will never know. And then it may be too late.

Sometimes enthusiasm leads to failure to perform sufficient due diligence. People become so enamored of the process and the prospect of doing a deal that they want to paper over the cracks that may be appearing. It's good to keep things in perspective and not let small issues blow up a deal. But, by the same token, if there are major issues that shouldn't be overlooked, people must acknowledge them.

In other words, a little momentum can be a dangerous thing. If you are a public company and you have announced that you are looking at a target company, you have your board of directors geared up to approve it, you are geared up, and it's very difficult to apply the brakes. You are a naysayer if you want to stop. That kind of unbridled momentum was typical of the 1980s. People had the money, they said they were going to do a certain deal, and they didn't want to look for reasons not to do the deal. At Premdor, we have learned through experience that some of the best deals we have done are the ones we never closed.

Tying the Knot

Throughout the due diligence process, you build your comfort level in the hopes that by the closing date, you will feel confident that tying the knot is the right thing to do. Thus, knowing when to say "No," and having the strength of your convictions, is equally as important as knowing when to proceed.

It is important to remember throughout the due diligence process that no deal is perfect. During the process, you continually seek corroboration of the information you have received—or contradiction of it. If there are skeletons in the closet, it's up to your team to find them. But at a certain point, you have to stop. Weighing all the pros and cons, and knowing as much as it's practical to know, you've either reached a comfort level you can live with or you haven't. At that point, it comes down to your decision and the amount of risk versus reward.

It's not uncommon to hear of companies that, time after time, never achieve the comfort level they need when trying to expand. The risk of going ahead always seems too great. These are companies that too often miss opportunities. No matter how much due diligence you perform, and how much planning and forecasting you undertake, there will always be some risk inherent in an acquisition or merger. You can't eliminate it, but through the due diligence process you can try to minimize it.

Bear in mind that helping you minimize risk is the job of your lawyers, accountants, and other professional advisors. They are there to help you clarify and understand matters involving the acquisition or merger and to ensure that your position is protected. Managing these professionals is an important part of controlling the preacquisition or premerger process. It's vital to ensure that all your professionals are undertaking all the tasks they should be undertaking—and that they are doing so on a timely basis. When the process is allowed to drag on, second thoughts begin to take shape, and the process can fall apart. Your professional advisors need to understand that this is a business deal, not a quest for perfection.

They—and you—also need to be very clear about the fact that *you* are the one who ultimately makes the "Go" or "No-go" decision. They do not make the decision for you. They are not taking the risk—you are. You know your business and your industry better than they do, and you are likely to think more strategically about it than they are. It is your judgment call. Your willingness to take responsibility for making the final decision is critical. As noted, some of the best deals Premdor has done are deals we walked away from. On the other hand, we also have been in acquisition negotiations during which our lawyers and some of our corporate officers were ready to walk away in utter frustration. It took a strong conviction on my part to make sure that the deal went ahead.

Working to Make the Marriage Last

Like a civil marriage, a corporate marriage is not necessarily successful simply because the two parties were able to negotiate their way to the altar—it's successful because of all the work put into making the union last. Thus, once you've tied the knot and signed the documents to formalize your corporate marriage, your real work begins. Successfully getting through the months immediately following the joining of the two companies is often the most difficult part of doing an acquisition or merger. This can be especially true in the case of a merger, when there is uncertainty about the future direction of the merged company, and employees may be confused about where their loyalties should lie. If those in charge have not planned for this transitional period, or are too worn out from working to make the marriage a reality, then things can quickly fall apart. The high corporate divorce rate indicates that many chief executive officers, and their teams, need to better prepare for conjugal life.

Preparation for life after your acquisition or merger begins, of course, with planning. In order to get off on the right foot, it's critical that your plan focuses on three key issues:

1. People.

2. Communications.

3. Timing.

Reassure Your People

Whether you expand by acquisition or merger, the union will have the immediate effect of making people within the organizations nervous. One of your most important tasks after tying the knot will be to bring direction and reassurance to the people in your organization.

Many management issues will have been dealt with during the engagement period. For example, if two companies are merging, the CEOs of the firms will agree upon who heads up the new organization before the deal is finalized. Also, top management probably will be involved in some reorganizational planning. In the period immediately after the corporate marriage takes place, it will be the employees who need attention. Suddenly, they find themselves working for a new company. How and where do they fit in? Where do their loyalties lie—with the old management, if it is staying on, or with the new management? What about potential job loss, transfers, or plant closings?

If you expand through acquisition, the issue of who bought whom is clear-cut. With a merger, however, uncertainty levels tend to be higher as people toy with each other about where the power lies, which company is the dominant partner, and who "won" in the negotiations. Either way, the rumor mill will begin churning. In many cases, after all, you'll be acquiring or merging with a competitor about whom uncomplimentary stories may have been circulating in your company or vice versa. Now, overnight, employees must deal with the fact that "they are us and we are them."

Communicate the Long-Term Plans of the New Company

At this point, your communications plan can make or break the transition period. Clear definition of roles and goals within the new organization is a must. And a case for the change must be made. If you are involved in a merger, the new CEO must be recognized as soon as the deal is finalized. Immediately after the documents are signed in either an acquisition or merger, it becomes the CEO's job to communicate the long-term plans of the company to the employees and to manage the initial shock control. Throughout the transition period, officers of the company also must devote their time and energy to the communications effort. Failure to do so will mean that company will not perform to its fullest ability. Failure to get the communications message straight also can cause problems. For example, one vice president may be under the impression that a certain manager will be staying on at a certain location, and tell the manager so, when, in fact, the plan calls for that person to be transferred. Conflicting stories can do more than cause post-marriage problems—they also can lead to lawsuits.

Remember, too, that one of the reasons to expand through an acquisition or merger is that it gives you instant management. If you are buying the company or joining forces with it in order to get good management, the last thing you want to do is lose that asset. Getting people to be on the team is critical to your success.

Pay Attention to Timing: Set a New Direction Quickly

After you've tied the knot, timing is everything. Trying to maintain the status quo for a "honeymoon" period is too risky. Rather, new direction must come quickly in order to reduce uncertainty not only within the company but also in the marketplace. Moving slowly or waiting until things "settle down" only gives your competitors an opening to take market share away from you. If customers perceive that the company is adrift, they will take their business elsewhere.

Unless you begin immediately to try to reduce the apprehension and fear within your organization, performance problems also can build. Subsequently, they may take a long time to unwind.

While decisive action is important, it is also important to note that it is often not possible to reach your ultimate goal for the new company the day after the acquisition or merger is finalized. There is nothing wrong with implementing your plan in steps. For example, you may set goals for the first six months and then move on to your plan for the next six-month period, and so on.

Implementing the Internal Plan

One of the most direct ways to ease uncertainty and communicate the new corporate identity is to consider reorganizing the business. For example, the CEO of a now-expanded manufacturing company may decide that it is most effective to restructure the company into a manageable number of operating divisions, each with its own general manager who has bottom-line responsibility. Employees, directed to one of the new divisions, then know to whom they are reporting and where they fit in.

As CEO, it is your job to ensure that managers and supervisors are fully aware of changes to the organization and reasons for the changes. Thus, meetings bringing them together will form an important part of your agenda. Making it clear that long-term survival in the industry, not short-term savings, motivated the marriage and explaining corporate objectives and goals will give managers and supervisors a message that they can carry back to their divisions and those who report to them. In this way, the new vision of the company will filter through the entire organization. It is important for this vision to be widely, clearly, and repeatedly broadcast throughout the company in order to create a sense of direction, unity, and shared goals for everyone. If all regional divisions know that they are key players in making the company a strong national and international competitor, then they know the point of the acquisition or merger, the point of organizational changes, and the point of their redefined roles. If employees know that the company is striving to be a low-cost producer and it is explained to them how the acquisition or merger helps the company achieve that goal, then they also will be able to see how their daily actions and decisions fit into the overall corporate picture.

At the same time, the flow of information has to be two-way. The CEO and senior managers have to ensure that good and complete information is coming back to them. If any of the divisions are having problems adapting to the new organization or are not convinced about the wisdom of the company's new direction, the problems must be sorted out. Always bear in mind that while two CEOs may agree that an acquisition or merger is a great idea, if no one below them believes in it, the marriage can't possibly be successful.

As noted earlier, after making a major acquisition of three companies in 1991, Premdor immediately initiated a quarterly newsletter to employees. Called *Passages*, the premier issue came out soon after the acquisitions were completed. It had articles on our expansion, people, promotions, new products, and trade shows.

As the company has grown, so has the newsletter. Each issue is now filled with contributions from all our divisions. Since we acquired a door manufacturer in Bordeaux, France, in 1993, we now also have European circulation and content. The foreign connection causes a lot of interest and excitement among our North American employees. But more than that, it makes them proud that their company is a global competitor.

=====

Implementing the External Plan

You also will have to deal with the uncertainty of your suppliers and customers. There are a number of ways to let your clients know about the new company. Many companies find it useful to hold group luncheons to introduce the new corporation. In addition, some companies find that corporate videos are useful in post-acquisition or post-merger presentations to clients. You might also consider adopting a new corporate logo and new corporate colors.

Regardless of the type of presentation you choose to make to customers, ensure that it passes on a clear message about the strengths of the expanded company. For example, if one of the reasons you expanded was to be able to provide better service, reinforce that message with your clients. And, once again, do it as soon as possible—it's in your interests to keep them informed.

Monitoring the Corporate Marriage

Follow-up is essential to the continued success of your corporate marriage. Thus, your expansion will include two critical elements:

1. Monitoring your financial information.

2. Meetings among senior staff.

As discussed in Chapter 2, good financial reporting is one of the core resources necessary for expansion—without it you will lose control of your growth. When you merge with or acquire another company, you must ensure that you have financial information on a timely basis. All the steps outlined in Chapter 2 for using financial information as a control apply.

Part of measuring how well you are doing is talking to people. As CEO, ongoing meetings with senior staff, divisional managers, and supervisors will form a significant part of your monthly schedule. If you have operations in more than one location, this may mean an increase in your travel time. Or you may consider holding management meetings bringing people from all your divisions together. If you can combine this with some sort of social outing, so much the better.

PART THREE
Expanding Abroad

CHAPTER 6

Analyze Your Position and Assess Your Export Potential

In this chapter you will learn how to:

◆ Determine whether you are ready to make the commitment to export.

◆ Determine whether you have exportable products.

◆ Begin planning a strategy for going global.

◆ Begin to plan for managing the demands that exporting will place on your company.

Can You Afford Not to Export?

In the previous chapters, you have read about beating the competition and growing successfully by developing a defensive strategy. That strategy is based on staying close to your customers, reassuring them that your proximity means better service, and expanding your product line to give them more reasons to buy from you. And you have read about mounting an offense by expanding into new domestic markets—shipping from New York to California, for example—and forming alliances. If such strategic moves have enabled you to carve out a strong position in your domestic markets, your next step should be to explore exporting.

If your company's experience is typical, your first taste of the effects of globalized trade and increasing international competition has been on the receiving end, through a foreign product that is as well-designed and as well-made as yours. Your customers can buy it for less and your new offshore competitor promises service that will match, if not outdo, yours.

It's a fact of life that, no matter how strong your current position, your domestic market could shrink within the next ten years, if it hasn't already, because of foreign competition (see the fact sheet in Figure 6-1). And that's why going on the offensive is an effective strategy for maximizing your full potential. By entering your foreign competitor's, or someone else's, market, you are taking action in the changing marketplace rather than just reacting to it and potentially losing ground by default.

Figure 6-1. **Global facts for the potential exporter.**

1. You are facing more competition at home—and more of it is from offshore players than ever before.

2. The small, regional markets and protective tariffs that characterized trade after World War II are rapidly becoming a thing of the past.

3. It's not only foreign giants that export, it's small- and medium-sized companies, too.

4. The globalization of trade, aided by high-tech communications and rapid, accessible travel and transport, affects virtually every industry.

5. For companies in Asia, Europe, Scandinavia, and elsewhere, doing business internationally is simply an integral part of doing business.

6. North American markets are now mature, highly competitive, relatively low-margin markets.

7. More than 95 percent of the world's population lives outside the United States.

8. With implementation of the North American Free Trade Agreement among the United States, Canada, and Mexico, a tariff-free trading bloc with 360 million people has been created.

9. Harmonization of regulations and standards in the European Economic Community means that exporters can efficiently market to the world's largest trading bloc rather than having to market country by country.

10. Moves to decentralize control of most Eastern European economies are opening rich opportunities for foreign companies ready to sell in those vast markets.

No matter what type of industry you are in, all of the statements in Figure 6-1 are true. And for many business owners, these facts lead to two inescapable conclusions:

1. Each year, doing business at home is and will continue to become tougher.

2. Now more than ever, profitable opportunities abroad shouldn't be overlooked.

What Exporting Can Do for You

The Rewards

We began exporting doors to the United Kingdom in 1983 for a very simple reason—the demand for doors in western Europe was as high, if not higher, than the demand for doors in North America. Along the way, we've had to deal with (among other things) production staff who protested having to make doors any other size than the size they were used to making, and shipping conditions that created problems including warping of our doors.

Why did we bother? You could say that's a $10 million question because that's the value of the doors that we now ship to the United Kingdom each year. As an added attraction, our foothold in the U.K. market and the experience we've gained have also opened doors to markets in France and elsewhere in Europe. The size of the door markets on foreign shores—and the protection we gain from being in more than one market—makes it all worthwhile.

Some of the obvious *advantages* of exporting are:

♦ Your market is diversified—if domestic sales are flat, foreign sales can boost the bottom line, or vice versa.

♦ You can diversify product lines and/or gain a new lease on life for products that are mature in the North American market.

♦ There is potential to increase the volume of production at your existing plants.

♦ You open yourself to opportunities to source products and raw materials from foreign suppliers at lower cost than at home—becoming a low-cost producer helps you compete better not only abroad but also at home.

♦ You will be encouraged to improve your products and processes—foreign customers are often tougher on you than domestic customers; their demands will make you become tougher on yourself and more competitive.

♦ You will gain increased exposure to new ideas, new people, and new competition—these make your company more efficient and innovative in the long run.

What Exporting Can't Do for You

Some of the *disadvantages* or difficulties of exporting include:

♦ Results are long term, not instant.

♦ Planning the process properly takes time, money, and effort—the onus is on you, as CEO, to play a major role in getting the export venture off the ground.

♦ Convincing employees that accommodating change is worth the effort can be difficult.

♦ Attitudes toward business and a different pace of doing business in many foreign markets can be frustrating if you and your employees are not prepared.

♦ Possible product modifications, increased paperwork and shipping costs, and potentially longer collection periods for foreign sales will affect your current operations.

What Opportunities Exist?

As you weigh the advantages and disadvantages, and the benefits and risks, of exporting, it's important to keep in mind how markets around the world are changing.

For example, look at the potential markets in your own backyard. With the signing of the North American Free Trade Agreement (NAFTA) among the United States, Canada, and Mexico, the largest free-trading area in the world has been created. American and Canadian companies, which already operated under a free-trade agreement, now also gain tariff-free access to the Mexican market—a market that contains 85 million people and is on this continent, not thousands of miles away across the ocean.

Given that Mexico's economy is currently growing at the fastest rate in the country's history, significant opportunities await those poised to take them. What more sensible way to develop strong exports than to start selling to a market with no duty barriers? And why stop there? As North American companies get better at exporting south of the border, Mexico can serve as a stepping-stone to other markets and opportunities, for example, those in Latin America.

Or look at the markets in the Far East. They have long been seen as closed shops for all but the giants, such as Coca-Cola. However, those markets are shifting rapidly. Once driven by exports, they are now being driven by increasing demand for imports. Many smaller Pacific Rim customers would be more comfortable dealing with foreign companies that are the same size they are. And distributors and trading companies in the Orient are extremely eager for exclusive lines. The entrepreneurial style and energy typical of North American companies promises to be a real source of strength for those taking the initiative to carve out a niche in these dynamic markets.

The point is:

♦ There are many foreign markets in which North American companies can carve out a profitable niche if they are willing to plan properly.

♦ Carving out a niche is something you've done before.

♦ Whether you've introduced a new product to your current market or have taken an existing product to a wider market domestically, you've basically gone through the process.

♦ Therefore, exporting, even to markets in the Far East, shouldn't be frightening.

The Challenge of Commitment

Yet, no matter how accurately you target a foreign market or how aggressively you pursue sales there, you won't succeed in the long run unless you are also willing to make a major commitment of three resources:

1. Time

2. Money

3. Effort

You've got to back up your venture with complete commitment—commitment to long-term results. In order to make money, you have to be willing to spend money—and time. Without sufficient preparation, research, resources, and patience, you'll be wasting both your time and your money.

Planning the Exporting Process

Any company, large or small, that is considering going global must take the time to learn the route. No matter where your target market eventually lies, the same three steps will lead you there. You must:

1. Analyze your position and assess your potential, as discussed in this chapter.

2. Undertake thorough research and fact-finding, as discussed in Chapter 7.

3. Develop and implement an effective export plan, as discussed in Chapter 8.

Ignore a step along the way and you're jeopardizing your success. International highways and shipping lanes are littered with the corpses of companies that thought they could take shortcuts.

As indicated, your first step in exploring exporting is to take stock. You must have a clear vision of where your company stands today before you move forward into foreign markets tomorrow. Thus, you must take the time to consider how exporting will affect your existing business, whether it will strengthen the position of your business, and whether it fits in with your long-term goals. At this initial stage, then, the most important tasks of any CEO who is considering going global include:

◆ Performing a corporate self-evaluation.

◆ Learning the foreign competition that has invaded your market.

◆ Assessing the types of changes your business must undergo and how you'll manage change within your organization.

◆ Thinking about how to get everybody onside, with top management taking the lead.

Look in the Mirror

It's not enough to say that you're going to start exporting. Your business has to be able to actually do it. And that means taking a long, hard look at your organization before you leap.

No matter what type of industry you are in, common factors will help you determine whether you are in a position to support an export venture. Go through the checklist in Figure 6-2 to get an idea of how your company stacks up.

Figure 6-2. **The exporter's fitness test—corporate checklist.**

	Yes	No
1. Is your company meeting the demand for its products and services in the domestic market?	☐	☐
2. Does your company have an enviable track record at home?	☐	☐
3. Has your company been in business several years, and has it successfully managed domestic growth?	☐	☐
4. Does your company have a strong capital base and the financial resources to back an export venture over the long term?	☐	☐
5. Does your company have a good relationship with your bankers?	☐	☐
6. Will an export venture jeopardize current domestic business?	☐	☐
7. Does your company have the personnel to handle new, foreign markets *and* also have good managers and staff capable of keeping the home fires burning?	☐	☐
8. Do you and your team have the patience to wait years for your export program to work?	☐	☐
9. Does your company have the production capacity to meet increased demand for your existing product(s)?	☐	☐
10. Does your company have the production capability to meet demand for a modified version of your product(s)?	☐	☐

If you answered "No" to any of the questions in Figure 6-2, your company probably needs to build up additional strength domestically before plunging into exporting. If you answered "Yes" to all the questions, your company is probably in a good position to broaden its horizons. In order to begin assessing your foreign potential, consider the following issues, most of which are dealt with in greater detail in Chapters 7 and 8.

What product do you think you will export?

♦ Your best-known product.

♦ Your most profitable product.

♦ A marginal product with a better chance of succeeding in a market where competition is not as fierce.

♦ A product that is mature in your domestic markets, but might be in high demand in developing markets.

Your first inclination may be to consider your most successful and most profitable product, but this may not be the wisest choice. Likely, your target market will dictate your final choice. You may discover, for example, that one of your marginal products can be marked up aggressively in a particular foreign market, while in that same market the price of your most profitable domestic product would have to be slashed.

In evaluating which product to export, you may have to decide on a country-by-country basis, and factors other than maximizing profit may play a part. You may eventually decide that you can live with lower profit margins in order to gain access to a particularly large target market or in order to keep your production facilities running at top capacity. The effect of exchange rates on your prices will also be a consideration.

How do you think you will market your product?

♦ Are you prepared to alter your successful product so it will fly in another country?

♦ Are you prepared to alter the way you normally market and service the product?

♦ If you have always sold directly, are you prepared to work with an export agent?

♦ Are you prepared to revamp your advertising?

When you export, you have to think in terms of where the product will be used, not in terms of where it's manufactured. Premdor's Canadian-made FastFit pre-hung doors may be hot sellers in Toronto, but will they be appropriate in Korea? We'll undoubtedly have to change the measurements. Will we also have to change the materials? The hardware?

When we first began selling doors in France, we were told in no uncertain terms that they were flimsy because they didn't weigh as much as doors made there. Ours contain a corrugated, glue-impregnated cardboard interior, while doors manufactured in France have a particle board interior. Ours are as strong, but theirs are heavier. We talked to a number of buyers and decided that the weight difference could become a problem, so we made our doors for the French market heavier by adding some particle board. This involved various changes at one of our plants, but not enough to interfere with our markups to French buyers.

There is nothing wrong with altering or modifying your product for foreign markets, but you will have to take the time to satisfy yourself that changes are really necessary. If you begin to sell in a variety of foreign markets and have a different version of your product for each market, the potential for problems and confusion is magnified. How will you ensure that production specifications and inventory for each market are not mixed up? Will you have to begin to source a wide variety of new materials? Will servicing instructions differ for each market?

Modifications that simplify your product, improve its quality, and make it more universal are probably the only types of changes you should consider.

Dealing with export agents has its advantages and disadvantages. On the plus side, an export agent or export trading company can help you get that all-important first sale, thus demonstrating that there are buyers for your product in your target market. On the other hand, the fee you pay the export agent will eat into your profit, and you may have to agree to an exclusive contract with the agent.

As for revamping advertising, your marketing department may find that simplifying its copy for foreign translation is a great exercise. It can help improve communication and encourage ideas about how to improve copy and campaigns for your current domestic market.

Are you prepared to adapt to the following in foreign markets?

♦ Different measurements.

♦ Distinctive safety standards.

♦ Different labeling or packaging requirements.

♦ Greater government regulation, and a variety of other restrictions.

♦ Fewer or no regulations, such as patent and copyright laws, to protect your product in foreign markets.

♦ A new taxation regime.

———————

When we began to manufacture doors for the French market, we were confronted with a number of minor changes that were required under French building standards. For the French part of our runs, we had to make a number of relatively slight adjustments, every one of which was met by some degree of protest in the plant, along the lines of: "If we have been making perfectly good doors for years and they have always sold, why should we change now?" Of course we weren't going to have much luck persuading the French to change their building standards, so our doors had to change.

———————

To a large extent, information on issues such as safety standards and labeling and packaging requirements can be obtained from trade offices at the nearest consulate or embassy of the country to which you wish to export. For American companies interested in exporting, the U.S. Department of Commerce also has detailed information on foreign markets. Canadian companies should turn to External Affairs and International Trade Canada or the federal Export Development Corporation. These U.S. and Canadian federal departments can also provide leads on where to obtain government funding to help with researching your export venture.

Are you prepared to "re-learn" your market?   There are two types of markets you can go after if you are exporting. One is the market in which the type of product you make isn't currently sold. The other is the market that is already using the type of product you manufacture.

If the type of product you make isn't sold in a potential foreign market, how will you convince people to buy it? If the product is already familiar to consumers, how will you convince them that your brand is better than others? You'll not only have to know your product inside out, you'll also have to know the competition's just as well.

Trade shows are an invaluable source when you are trying to answer these types of questions and gather information. So are domestic and foreign trade publications that specialize in information about your industry.

Do you have the time, the money, and the resources to commit to the program? Are you prepared to take what may be the most risk you've taken since you started up your business?   You'll get a better idea of the resources that must be devoted to an export program when you begin mapping out a detailed business plan and budget. But right now, you should be able to ballpark a few numbers and make a quick determination about whether the cost of exporting is feasible or whether it seems to be out of the question. Then ask yourself if you're being penny-wise and pound-foolish.

Try thinking of your export strategy as a capital investment. If you purchase a $1 million machine that helps you make $400,000 a year, you have an investment that will pay off handsomely in less than three years. Similarly, if you commit the money and time to thoroughly researching, planning, and budgeting for exporting, your investment should pay off. Can you still afford not to do it?

Do you know if you can deliver your goods successfully to the new market?   It may not be enough to add on simple transportation expenses to the cost of selling your product.

———

You'll recall that we had problems with doors warping en route to the United Kingdom. Some probing revealed that humidity in the container ships was a real problem. The solution was easy—it was all in adapting the packaging we do at our plants. This did not add to the weight of the doors and so did not increase transportation costs. But it did add to the cost of production. However, our markups were adequate to cover the unexpected expense.

———————

You also will have to research the advantages, and cost, of using customs brokers, freight forwarders, and export agents. You can buy containers for shipping, but should you rent them instead? Insurance will be an issue too. However, because you are now simply at the stage of thinking about exporting and assessing your state of readiness, you do not yet need to worry about getting detailed information on these issues.

Do you know what you are good at and where you will need help? Are you willing and able to be flexible?   If customers in Montreal are used to once-a-week deliveries, but in your home market of Vermont, you ship only once a month, can you adapt? Credibility is the hardest thing to establish in an export market, and the most difficult to maintain.

Are you personally prepared for the exporting challenge?   In the process of assessing your corporate readiness to export, it's essential to reflect on your own, personal state of readiness to handle an export venture. With or without the help of a management team, nine in ten CEOs shoulder most of the burden of getting their company's export effort up and running. Are you ready to handle issues such as those outlined in Figure 6-3 on the following page?

Learn from Foreign Competitors

After taking a long, hard look at your corporate and personal situations, you need to begin to look outward again—this time at the competition in your own backyard, specifically, at your foreign competition. Who are they and how did they gain a foothold?

If you can thoroughly analyze how foreign competitors successfully entered your market here at home, you may begin to sow the seeds of your

Figure 6-3. **The exporter's fitness test—CEO's personal checklist.**

	Yes	No
1. Do you have an open mind and are you willing to learn about new countries and new cultures?	☐	☐
2. Do you believe that "the way we do things at home" is not necessarily the way to do things abroad?	☐	☐
3. Are you willing to learn another language?	☐	☐
4. Do you have the stamina to take on a heavier workload?	☐	☐
5. Are you prepared to travel extensively?	☐	☐
6. Are you ready to delegate and to let someone else make critical business decisions in your absence?	☐	☐
7. Are you patient?	☐	☐
8. Are you willing to stand in a booth at international trade shows to promote your product?	☐	☐

The only acceptable answer to these questions is "Yes."

own strategy abroad. At the same time, you can begin to assess whether their home market holds potential for you. Of course, the conditions facing you in foreign markets will not always be the same as those facing your competitors in North America. But a number of the difficulties that your competitors encountered, such as foreign languages, differing consumer expectations, fluctuation in currency exchange rates, and different tax systems, will be the same ones you encounter. When you consider your competitors' strategies, think about the following issues:

1. *Exactly how did they begin competing? Was it . . .*

   ♦ Price?

   ♦ Service?

   ♦ A superior product?

   ♦ Better engineering or design?

2. *How did they enter your market?*

   ◆ By selling directly to distributors?

   ◆ Through an agent?

   ◆ Did they set up a brand new shop?

   ◆ Did they start with one product or more than one?

   ◆ How did they make their presence felt initially?

   ◆ How large, expensive, or comprehensive was their campaign to enter your market?

3. *What did your customers initially think of your competitors?*

   ◆ What do they think of them now?

   ◆ What makes them buy your competitor's product as well as yours?

   ◆ What makes your customers' customers buy the product?

   ◆ How did the foreign competition adapt to the North American way of doing business?

   ◆ How deep do you think their pockets were initially?

And don't forget to look at the competitors who failed. You probably can remember a few, but your customers will have lots of stories. They are the ones who bought the product in the first place and then had to deal with the new kid on the block mixing up orders, missing deadlines, losing a grip on quality, and maybe even disappearing. Ask, listen, and learn.

Prepare to Manage Change

Depending on the nature of your business, structural changes brought about by developing an export market could be minimal. Or they could reverberate throughout your organization, affecting everything from the way employees design, produce, inspect, and ship products, to the way you formulate your strategic plans.

C an your company cope with, or learn quickly how to adapt to, situations such as the following?

♦ When Premdor entered the market in France, our personnel department had to deal with its first employee resident outside Canada or the United States. That meant they had to research what benefits—such as sick pay, pensions, paid leave, bonuses, and parental leave—are typically offered in France, and at what level, before we negotiated a contract with our French employee. They also had to check our candidate's references. They were able to do these things with the help of our accounting and legal firms, both of which have specialists in international business. Once our French employee was onboard, the personnel department also had to set up systems for remitting payment to him and for remitting tax to the French government.

♦ Because we now had an office in France, our comptroller had to deal with a host of different accounting and tax regulations. Again, the international expertise and resources of our professional advisors were crucial.

♦ Shortly after we made our first sale in Spain, our contracts department opened a courier pouch one morning and found 50 very legal looking pages all in Spanish, which had to be dealt with in less than a week. Since contract law in Europe is quite different from that in the United States and Canada, assistance from a lawyer with expertise in international commercial law was essential. The bilingual contracts that we developed specify the exact contents of the order, price, payment terms, shipping terms, service and warranties, and liabilities, and we find that we usually can use them as the basis for contracts with buyers in countries other than Spain also.

♦ How we filled our initial European orders with the right kind of doors could take up a chapter by itself. On large orders with custom work involved, our plant managers often deal directly with customers. It's part of Premdor's service, and it results in the right doors being shipped the first time. We recently sent a plant manager from Toronto to Milan, Italy, for example, to meet directly with one of our customers. However, when we first dealt with overseas customers, the six-hour time zone difference, the different languages, different measuring systems, unusual specifications, and the European penchant for treating details such as the color of stain as an in-depth philosophical enquiry made life challenging for several months. As you'll read in the following pages, taking the time to foster commitment to the export program and to help employees understand how it would benefit them in the long run was an essential component in keeping patience levels at a maximum.

◆ When we began to ship doors to France, Spain, and other parts of Europe, we quickly realized each country has its own regulations governing labeling, documentation, shipment, and unloading of goods. We had to decide whether to make someone within the company responsible for learning about such regulations or to enlist the help of foreign freight forwarders. Putting the job in the hands of outside experts proved to be the best solution for us.

◆ Billing our new foreign customers demanded a great deal of patience in accounting, although we had learned from our contract experience and had quickly developed bilingual bills. Foreign exchange was another problem. We always sell in the domestic currency, not American dollars. Thus we had to learn about hedging against changes in the value of foreign currency.

◆ Along the way, we had to change a number of our computer programs and to find the cheapest way to phone, fax, and send documents to our European customers.

―――――――――

As your export market matures, other structural issues will inevitably crop up. However, it's never too soon to ask yourself how you'll handle some of the following:

♦ Will your company source supplies for your export products from existing suppliers or will you be expected to purchase some supplies in your export market?

♦ What effect will this have on your domestic products?

♦ What kind of professional help will you have to engage, here and overseas, as you become more involved with exporting?

♦ How much new infrastructure will be needed just to service the new export market?

♦ Who will be needed on staff to take care of problems that didn't exist before?

♦ How will you recruit help, here and overseas, that is familiar with your new markets?

♦ Will you eventually need to set up a new shop in your new territory?

Managing change in your business is as crucial to the success of your export program as finding the right product or right marketing strategy. Failure to manage change can affect more than the success of your export venture—it can threaten the health of your domestic operations. And failure to manage growth can have the same repercussions. As explained in Chapter 1, control is essential for long-term success.

Prepare to Foster Commitment

To implement the structural changes needed for your export program, you'll have to get a high level of commitment and cooperation at all levels in your organization, from the offices of management to the shop floor to the mail room.

Not everybody likes change. Most business owners do; that's why they are owners. Convincing all your employees to adopt the same attitude may be another story. If you are running a successful business, many of your staff are going to wonder why you are bothering to tamper with success.

You've got to take the lead, show that you are 100 percent behind the export program, and play a significant role in planning the venture. You've got to ensure that every employee who will be involved understands why the company is willing to commit substantial funds and energy to a project that may not see the light of day for several years and could be five or six years away from profit.

In North America, we're hooked on quick hits and fast results. Companies rise and fall based on their quarterly earnings. Most management teams love approving expenditures on big, million-dollar machines. They know that three months later, a shiny new, computer-driven piece of equipment that takes up half the plant floor will arrive and everyone will be very impressed.

Talk to management teams about approving $1 million to develop an export program, and the enthusiasm can be underwhelming. An export program isn't nearly as sexy as machinery, it's not tangible, and it may not produce results for five years.

Your people will respond fruitfully to the new direction the company is taking only if they are committed to it. You look upon your proposed exporting program as a challenge and a business necessity over the long term. Your attitude has to be communicated to your people, and they have to become infected by it. You know your staff and what motivates them best. Two guidelines for getting everyone onside are:

1. *Sell your staff on what you're sold on.* If the idea of exploring new frontiers by selling your product or service in another country is part of what motivates you, translate that excitement into terms that will be meaningful to your employees. If you believe that exporting will make your company better, show your employees how that will make them better at their jobs. For example:

- ◆ You may have to improve your product to make it more appealing to foreign customers. If this means that your production staff needs additional training or skills upgrading in order to better engineer your product, then everyone benefits.

- ◆ If you need to invest in better equipment in order to improve your product, your employees will benefit by learning to work with state-of-the-art technology.

◆ If you need to develop an improved database on each item you produce so that you can solve problems when a customer calls from Tokyo, then your customer service representatives will be able to do a better job, and your computer people will have improved their skills.

If your employees can meet the challenges of exporting, they'll experience personal rewards that will enhance their abilities and their careers. And they'll be better equipped to meet the challenges of the nineties.

2. *Sell your staff on bottom-line results.* If you are excited about exporting because it will add substantially to profits, think about instituting a long-term incentive program based on the success of your exporting program.

It's not enough, however, to work employees up into a short-lived frenzy. You must be sure you have the people onboard who can accommodate change and meet the challenges head-on. Before you commit more time and dollars to exploring a potential program, take the time to review your staff, at all levels, to see what kind of challenges they may face and what kind of commitment you'll be expecting from them.

◆ Senior management

◇ Consider putting them through the same export fitness test you took in Figure 6-3.

◆ Sales representatives

◇ Can they cope with increased paperwork?

◇ Do they have the initiative to develop new systems to accommodate new situations?

◇ Are they ready to learn at least the rudiments of another language or two?

◇ Are they ready for extensive travel to countries where travel isn't as easy as it is in North America and Europe?

♦ Systems personnel

◇ Does the company have the computer expertise to cope quickly with new situations?

◇ How successful have your systems people been in the past at innovation and at developing new systems to increase the efficiency and competitiveness of your business?

♦ Accounting personnel

◇ Are your people ready to develop new computer skills?

◇ Are they prepared to contribute to new accounting systems that will evolve rather than arrive in the office in perfect condition?

◇ Are they willing to take on the task of developing a cost system that provides the detailed information needed for international sales? For example, how will you know the effect on profitability of various modifications to your product for foreign markets? What prices do you need to charge to maintain your standard level of profit?

◇ Given that collections on foreign accounts regularly stretch out to 60 or 90 days, how will accounting track accounts and handle follow-up?

♦ Plant staff

◇ Are all levels of staff in your plant ready to accommodate a variety of major and minor changes, and are they prepared to shift gears as often as every few minutes?

As our export markets have expanded, new conditions have effected changes at every level in the business. The most difficult is at the most fundamental level—manufacturing. We make hundreds of different types of doors and the specifications change for each market, so that literally thousands of different doors come out of the plants each year. It required a sustained effort to encourage our staff to see that changeovers as often as every hour made sense.

═══════════

- ◆ Secretaries and clerks

  - ◇ Things are done differently in each and every country. Are staff prepared for these differences, and will they learn how to interpret them?

  - ◇ Little things count, too. Is your receptionist prepared to learn a few words in perhaps as many as half a dozen different languages?

- ◆ Outside advisors

  - ◇ Do they have the necessary expertise to offer you the best possible guidance as you deal with all the normal business problems in one or more foreign countries?

  - ◇ Do your current advisors have branches or good connections in your target country?

If you can anticipate the types of challenges your business will meet as you develop your export program, you'll be better able to judge how effectively your staff can deal with them, and you'll be better prepared to communicate the magnitude of the challenge to them. In the business world, the best surprise is no surprise. If your staff knows what's coming up and can prepare properly for it, your chances of success in the export market will increase significantly.

CHAPTER 7

Researching Potential Export Markets

This chapter will help you avoid the pitfalls of:

♦ Failing to search out the export market that represents the best opportunity for your company.

♦ Rushing into an export market before you are really ready.

At this stage, you need to start focusing your export plan by setting in motion a four-part process:

1. Targeting markets.

2. Developing a short list of target markets.

3. Gathering information.

4. Evaluating the risks and rewards.

What fuels progress from one step to the next is research and fact-finding. Your research and fact-finding mission has only one purpose—to gather enough information to enable you to make a decision. However, if you should decide not to enter the exporting fray, you should have gathered enough information from your research to bolster your defensive strategy on the home front against new competition. Most businesses that consider exporting also develop a much keener appreciation of how competitors might be entering their own market, now and in the future, and what they can do to hold on to their market share.

Targeting Markets

The classic advice given to businesses considering exporting is to find a market similar to their current market. The reasons are obvious. Why go to the expense and trouble of trying to sell in a market that is completely different when there is every possibility that you can successfully enter a market that is not too different from the one you successfully operate in now?

If you are an American company, why bother to search out potential markets in Europe or the Far East if you haven't yet looked north of the border to Canada? This is a market of 27 million people with a high standard of living. They speak English (French in Quebec) and follow most of the same business customs followed in the United States. Laws are similar, business conditions are similar, and the costs of entering the market are readily determinable. In other words, the risk factor is low. Canada is the United States' largest trading partner for precisely these reasons.

Nevertheless, you shouldn't ignore smaller or more distant markets that offer greater potential for sales and profit. Mature economies usually mean a competitive environment for most products and services. Unless you can enter with a definite price advantage, or your product or service is significantly different from what is currently available in the target market, and you can establish demand for it, you may be better off targeting developing countries.

If you are a Canadian company, the U.S. market south of the border is huge and tempting. It is more open now than it ever has been thanks to the North American Free Trade Agreement, but it is also the most competitive market in the world. Many Canadian companies have ventured south of the border with very poor results. Depending on the nature of your product or service, you may be better off casting your sights to other English-speaking markets such as the United Kingdom, Australia, or New Zealand, or to other French-speaking markets such as France.

But what about looking further afield to the Far East and countries such as Thailand or Singapore? Or what about looking south to Mexico or Chile? Or what about Eastern Europe? At first glance, the negatives of these markets may seem to outweigh the positives—different language, potential political instability, perhaps different units of measurement, currency uncertainty, different business customs, and high costs for shipping product. On the other hand, you may have a product that is in great demand in one of the markets. There also may be a variety of government programs in place in the target country, and even domestically, to encourage exporters such as you. These may range from free use of consultants to payment guarantees.

Targeting a developing country obviously involves more risk, but it also may involve a much larger reward in terms of profit and long-term sales. Comparing the risks and rewards of various markets is one of the major purposes of your fact-finding mission.

P remdor's first export market was the United States. Being able to truck our doors into a market that was ten times the size of Canada and still only a day's drive away made all the difference. The next offshore market we zeroed in on was the United Kingdom. We knew that freight wouldn't be a problem since there is already considerable trade between England and North America. The type of customer was similar. And perhaps most importantly, the size and type of product sold in England was very similar to the product we were selling in Canada and the United States. In our situation, it was much easier to export to the United Kingdom first rather than trying to enter other European markets where the product, measurements, and language differed.

Bear in mind, however, that upon having done your research on potential foreign customers, you may discover just how different two very similar countries, at least on the surface, can be, or how similar two very different countries are.

♦ The United States has the reputation of being one of the, if not the most, litigious country in the world. From a Canadian, British, or Australian perspective, the United States has earned the reputation. The courts in these other three countries simply are not used nearly as often or for the same reasons. Yet, on the surface, these four markets are similar in many other respects. However, legal obstacles or simple litigiousness can represent a sizeable cost of doing business in the United States, while a lack of such litigiousness can be a major attraction for doing business in Canada, the United Kingdom, or Australia.

♦ The same four countries have fairly sophisticated regulatory environments and consumer protection legislation in most of the same areas. But not in every area and certainly not in every area of the country. For example, air pollution legislation is still young in Great Britain, while the United States has extensive legislation, particularly in California. Consumer protection legislation is considered relatively mature in Canada, but might be considered to be only in its infancy compared to the state of California, which has reams of regulations for many consumer goods.

Developing a Short List of Target Markets

There are many criteria that go into developing a short list of target export markets. However, one stands out from all the rest—the type of customer to whom you'll be selling.

Look for Similar Customers

Ideally, you want to find a market in which your customers will be the same as those back home. If you normally sell to distributors and wholesalers, as does Premdor, you want to sell to distributors and wholesalers in your new market. If you primarily make a few sales to large accounts, you want to do the same thing in your new market. If one of the main methods of promoting your product is setting up alliances with your customers, you want to be able to operate the same way in your target market.

It bears repeating: If you change your customer base, you are essentially changing the nature of your business. If you sell to wholesalers or distributors, selling directly at retail to final users is an entirely different ball game. Financing these sales, servicing the customers, and making deliveries are all completely different in most cases. If you don't sell at retail in your domestic market, there is no reason to consider it in a foreign market. Your problems will only be compounded by trying to develop an entirely new customer base on foreign soil, and your exporting drive will be just that much harder to launch successfully.

Although Premdor's products are used in both the new home construction industry and for renovation, we do not sell directly to contractors. We sell to distributors or wholesalers, or directly to retail stores or chains. As we developed our export markets in the United States, the United Kingdom, France, Mexico, Korea, Japan, and other countries, selling to the same customer base was the number one criterion as we explored potential markets. We are in the business of selling to distributors. We are not in the business of selling to contractors.

Hand in hand with finding a market with similar customers is finding a market where the distribution network is similar. In North America, we take for granted the typical selling chain that goes from manufacturer to distributor or wholesaler to retailer—although the emergence of warehouse-style stores in many sectors means that the line is rapidly blurring between distributor or wholesaler and retailer. We also take for granted our highly computerized systems for ordering, inventory, and shipping. This is not the way business is done in every part of the world. For example, in a number of countries in the Far East, trading companies dominate the landscape. These are essentially middlemen who may handle financing, sales, distribution, and even service. Unless you associate yourself with such a trading company, you may find it impossible to tap into the market in the particular country. Therefore, you either have to adapt or look for another market. Whether you choose to adapt is dependent on all the other criteria that go into making the decision on the appropriate target market.

Evaluate Pricing, Demand, and Competition

It goes without saying that how well you can price your product or service determines how successful your foray into exporting will be. In some instances, you will be competing with similar products or services. In such cases, customers in the target market are convinced your type of product or service is good, and they are already buying products similar to yours. But they are buying them from established sellers, not from you. These established sellers will do everything they can with their prices and service to discourage you from entering their territory. Essentially, you must be able to compete directly on price or you won't survive. Demand for your product or service and the nature of your competition will determine your pricing. Of course, your pricing must be competitive. In most situations, pricing actually will have to be better than the local sellers' prices in order to entice buyers to switch their accustomed buying habits. But, at the same time, you will have to establish a bottom line below which there is no point in pursuing a market further.

Competing on service is extremely difficult if you are just entering a market. It usually demands that you have made a number of sales and have some type of track record in the particular market. You have to give potential customers some concrete reasons to change suppliers. The fact that you offer top-notch service in your domestic market probably won't cut it in a highly competitive foreign market.

On the other hand, an Australian company selling into a small developing market, for example Chile, may discover little or no competition there. The competitors they would encounter in large markets, such as the United States, have not entered Chile. Thus, the company may be able to price its product or service much more favorably than it could in the United States and achieve much higher profit margins, despite the many other costs of doing business in Chile that would not be encountered in the United States.

As an exporter, you may be introducing a new product or a significantly different product into your target market. Whatever the level of competition, you now will have to create demand for your product or service. Creating demand for a new or different type of product in an unfamiliar market is generally much more risky than selling a known good in a competitive market and competing primarily on price. Of course, the rewards for success may be much greater.

In this type of exporting situation, you may discover that you have the entire market to yourself, at least for the time being. If you export to a smaller developing country where there are no products similar to yours, for example, it may be relatively easy to create demand although your potential customer base may be fairly small. You also might be able to establish a niche in a developed country that, for one reason or another, simply is not being filled by local sellers.

P remdor encountered exactly that type of niche when it identified the French market as a potential exporting destination. Builders and remodelers in France are accustomed to using a lot of solid wood doors. Premdor's moulded wood doors are targeted to the same new construction and renovation markets, are aesthetically appealing to consumers in those markets, and are less expensive. The demand was there for a product that was not previously available. We simply had to satisfy that demand.

Of course, each type of exporting situation comes with its own degree of risk. Finding an area of the world where you can fill a profitable niche sounds attractive and, on the surface, appears to carry little risk. However, usually a host of other factors raise the risk stakes considerably. Otherwise your competition would have found that market long ago. It's a small world and getting smaller every day.

It is essential that you investigate final consumer demand for your product or service. Your customers, who may be distributors or even retailers, may express great interest in your product, but this isn't necessarily a reflection of demand in your target market.

Consider Economic Factors

Too many potential exporters give short shrift to the economic realities of their potential target markets. They look at possible currency problems or legal entanglements, but ignore the nature of the economy in which they plan to do business. Generally, a market will have more potential for sales, growth, and profit if it is a growing economy. But growth, or potential growth, should not be your only yardstick. You must also closely assess your industry and the related factors that contribute to sales. When we were researching the door market in France, for instance, we went through exactly the same exercise that we go through annually in the United States and Canada. We reviewed general economic activity in France and then we looked closely at current and historical levels of home starts, new house sale data, and renovation activity.

It should come as no surprise that the same factors you painstakingly assess at home periodically in order to budget and plan for the coming years are the same factors that you should be looking at in your target market. Most of the statistics you need should be readily available in developed countries. The numbers may be harder to come by in developing countries, but generally you should be able to find help to marshal your data through government agencies, international accounting or law firms, professional export consultants, or trade associations.

Determine the Cost of Service

No matter what type of product or service you plan to export, it generally must be backed up by the same type of service you deliver to your customers at home. Doing this when the point of sale is a few hundred to a few thousand miles away, in a foreign country, can pose a problem.

There are exceptions however. If you plan to export a product that has a tremendous price advantage over its rivals in the target country, you may have a choice of downgrading your service and keeping the lower price or charging a higher price but providing more service. Your profit margins and ability to stay in the market over the long term will generally dictate how you approach this decision.

In most situations, however, the reputation that you built at home and on which you are counting to ease access to your target market must be maintained. This means shipping the best quality product each and every time and ensuring that it arrives at your customer's doorstep in perfect condition. There probably will be no point in repairing defective goods that have arrived in the target country. Shipping them back home or sending a repair team to that country may not make economic sense.

Providing top-notch service can be a significant cost of any exporting venture. If you are shipping 10,000 miles instead of 10 miles, there are days when it seems that a thousand more things can go wrong. And every mistake costs money.

Calculate Freight and Landed Cost

Getting a quote for shipping your product to a town 100 miles away is an easy matter. You can generally rely on that quote and build it accurately into your cost equations as you are doing your budgeting. You also can get a quote on how much it *might* cost to ship your product to Europe or the Far East. But if you haven't done it before, you probably won't know exactly what the quote means or how the quote can be used to determine your total shipping costs or the costs of landing your product on a potential customer's doorstep. Any of the following could have a large impact on that final cost:

◆ Packing at home for shipping.

◆ Domestic costs for getting your product into a container.

◆ Domestic cost of getting the container to a point of departure.

◆ Unloading costs at your destination.

◆ Various port or point of entry costs.

◆ Duties or tariffs.

◆ Various taxes or levies imposed on your goods before they can be sold.

◆ Various costs of distributing your goods through a trading company or similar organization.

In other words, the cost of landing your goods is as much a product of the destination as it is a product of distance. The container costs for shipping 10,000 miles may be double the cost of shipping 5,000 miles, yet that 5,000 mile shipment could cost twice as much as the 10,000 mile shipment after everything is added up. Unless you are shipping to a market with which you are familiar, it usually will pay to obtain the services of an international trade consultant familiar with shipping to your target markets. Knowing the business customs of the country can often be more important than knowing the freight rates.

Watch Out for Other Factors

Depending on the nature of your product or service, a host of other factors may be just as important or more important than those just discussed.

Language.   It's an oversimplification to say that the international language of business is English. Yes, it is, but there are hundreds of languages of trade. Depending on the nature of your product or service, your target market, and your customers, you may be able to get away without doing business in the language of your target market. But more often than not, knowing the language will help establish your product in that market. If you want to export to France and plan to attend trade shows, you ought to have a command of French. You simply won't get as much out of the trade shows if you are restricted to speaking English. In any case, if you are facing direct competition in your target market from domestic producers or other exporters, service in the language of that country may be the factor that most customers use to determine from whom they will buy. Put the shoe on the other foot. Would you buy French goods from a salesperson who appeared on your doorstep speaking only French? You would probably hesitate, even though the goods appeared to be superior in quality to those you normally bought and were better priced.

When we started exporting to France, it became immediately apparent that it was to our advantage that Premdor was a Canadian company. We had been doing business in French and English for many years, and all our brochures, manuals, catalogues, and promotional material were printed in both French and English. Thus, language was not much of a barrier. Indeed, it has been an advantage for us to be able to use our French Canadian management to develop the French market.

Now that we are moving into Mexico, we are following the same pattern. We are using some of the Spanish-speaking sales and marketing people in our Texas plant to help advance our efforts in the Mexican market. We have also hired a Mexican who has lived in the United States to develop customer relationships and oversee our export development.

Measurement.   Most markets in the world are either on metric or imperial (British or American) measurement. Converting from one to the other may be as easy as altering the label on your goods or as difficult as retooling to make a product of a slightly different size. The related costs generally will dictate the markets into which you can export.

Packaging.   Many countries have a variety of packaging rules that differ slightly, or completely, from those in your home market. In North America, packaging rules vary from state to state and between the United States and Canada. For example, California has different rules for labeling ingredients on foodstuffs than those in force in other states, and Canadian rules are different again. As well, in Canada, labels generally must be bilingual (English and French, with text of both the same size so no bias is shown).

Labels must reflect the language, customs, and regulations of your target country. You may want to cover many bases and use international labeling, printed in seven or eight languages, as many European countries do on their exports. You also will have to do your research on whether your target market has environmental regulations, for example, stipulating that packaging must be recyclable.

Product modification.   While many North American products set the standard in many parts of the world, not everything goes over everywhere as well as it does in your home market. Something as basic as color could be a major stumbling block if you want to export to certain countries. What you think is beautiful in blue may turn off customers in your target market. What you perceive as lightweight may appear to be flimsy to your target customers. Generally, you have a choice. Convince your new customers that blue is beautiful or lightweight is good, or modify your product so that you can compete against other color products or heavy items. Both will involve considerable additional cost.

Advertising and promotion.   Don't make the mistake of thinking that you can promote your product or service in the target market exactly as you can at home. Many countries have only state television that does not accept advertising. Many have state-controlled newspapers that restrict advertising in some manner. And in many countries, social customs dictate a completely different approach to promoting your goods or service. In other words, don't count on using your domestic promotional campaign overseas. Dubbing a few slick lines over your current television ads or pasting over a foreign language blurb on your newspaper ads and brochures may result in developing more enemies than friends in the target country.

Regulatory regime.   This can be a minefield unless you have done your homework properly. There are stories galore about exporters thinking they had the perfect product for a particular market, landing that product on foreign shores, and being promptly told that they had better get it on the next boat out of the country. Markets that claim to be open for business may in fact be closed because of a regulatory labyrinth that no exporters are willing to enter. Most successful exporters use the services of international legal and regulatory specialists or have that type of expertise on staff.

Tax situation.   Exporting goods to another country generally will expose your company to a variety of taxes, from sales or commodity taxes such as the value added tax (VAT) in many European countries or the Goods and Services Tax (GST) in Canada, to income taxes to various other levies, including customs duties and other import tariffs. All add to the cost of exporting goods or services to the target country. Getting a handle on the tax situation in another country is a job for experts. Talk to your accountant, who should be able to steer you in the direction of the appropriate specialist. The larger accounting firms have extensive international connections.

Currency.   When you sell your product or service in a foreign country, chances are you will be paid in the currency of that country (it's obviously a real bonus if you can be paid in U.S. dollars or your own domestic currency). Converting that currency into domestic currency sometimes can be an adventure that you would rather not take part in. Currency values fluctuate. By the time you receive payment for your goods and services and convert those receipts back into dollars, you may receive more or fewer than expected because the value of the foreign currency has changed. Most businesses opt to hedge against changes in the value of foreign currency by buying futures, which ensure that their costs remain constant from the time of production to the time of payment.

Premdor's policy is always to hedge against the value of foreign currency, including the British pound. Our costs of selling doors in Britain is based on these hedged values. When the British pound was suddenly devalued from $2.80 Canadian to $1.90, the cost of our doors in terms of British pounds effectively went up by almost 40 percent. To maintain our margins, we would have had to increase the price of our doors immediately. We had no choice but to do so, but fortunately, our competition also had to increase prices. Our volumes and profits slipped a bit temporarily, but we retained our customers.

Local business customs.   Business is done in as many different ways around the world as there are countries and cultures. No matter what country you plan to export to, you will have to adapt to some degree. Generally, the more you adapt, the better your chances are of establishing a long-term exporting relationship with your target country and customers. Adapting, however, can be costly initially. In some countries, it may take a day or two of entertaining and socializing before your salespeople can even begin discussing the possibilities of a sale without offending your potential customers. In some countries, a definite "yes" or "no" is not part of the business lexicon. It's always "maybe," and you have to determine the level of interest implied in that "maybe."

Political situation.   No business likes to operate under a cloud of uncertainty, so you should certainly take some account of the political situation in your target markets. Any type of unrest means it's difficult to sell goods and perhaps even more difficult to collect payment. Dealing in countries with certain types of regimes may look profitable on the surface, but it may have a negative impact on your customers and investors back home. In your research and fact-finding, you should try to determine how the political climate of the target market will affect your chances for long-term success. Does the country have a tradition of political stability? Is anything likely to threaten that tradition? Does the market have a history of being "open for business"?

Investigate Payment Collection Methods

The last major point to bear in mind, and certainly not the least important, is determining exactly how you will be paid by your foreign customers and what recourse you have to enforce payment. While the arm of the law may be long in your home market, it generally doesn't stretch too effectively across international borders. Suing your customers for breach of contract or nonpayment in a foreign country is likely to be extremely expensive and, in many cases, frustrating. To protect payment for your deliveries, your choices essentially boil down to four:

1. Arrange to be paid in advance or in cash on delivery.

2. Arrange for guarantees of payment, such as letters of credit established by your customers that you draw on for payment. These letters of credit could be in foreign or domestic currency. Remember, however, that a banking letter of credit is only as strong as the bank supporting it.

3. Arrange insurance that in some manner guarantees payment of foreign receivables. Your federal, state, or provincial government may have special insurance programs in place that support exports. Such programs will help you set up insurance to guarantee payment of all or a portion of your receivables. You also may be able to find informal "insurance" or guarantee arrangements offered by specialized financial institutions.

4. Perform exceptionally careful and thorough credit checks of your potential customers.

The most common method used to ensure payment from foreign customers is the letter of credit. However, credit insurance is gaining ground in popularity. For those companies exporting across the border to Canada or the United States, factoring companies now are offering a credit guarantee service that smaller exporters are finding often works to their advantage. You perform your normal credit function, but for a fee, the factorer screens your customers and determines the credit risk. The factorer guarantees payment in the event of default, although you still do all the billing and collection. A secondary advantage of this arrangement is that your lenders now will look at all your receivables as acceptable collateral for working capital loans. Normally, banks won't include foreign receivables in their calculations, which impairs your ability to borrow. You also may be able to locate financial companies that specialize in guaranteeing letters of credit from less developed countries or other types of financing arrangements that the banks tend to shy away from.

Gathering Information

There are at least seven primary sources of information that you should consider tapping as you go through the process of developing a short list of target foreign markets. Chances are you will be exploiting all seven at the same time for various purposes.

1. *Local business, trade, or industry association.* Your industry or business association is primarily in the business of providing its members with information. And information on exporting is one of the topics on which most associations are up to date. Most associations are particularly geared toward providing valuable insights into exporting and information on products, customers, and existing manufacturers in potential markets.

2. *Government.* In most countries, the federal government has a variety of programs in place that encourage its companies to export. These programs range from information on doing business in virtually every country of the world to arranging for fact-finding trips to target countries to setting up financing for your first big sale. Much of the information and various services are free or available at a very nominal charge. You simply have to express an interest. State or provincial governments often provide a similar type of service. Local or municipal governments may perform the same types of service, although they tend to focus more heavily on attracting business to the area with various incentives such as municipal tax holidays.

3. *Networking.* The companies you do business with or are associated with are usually a gold mine of information. And, generally, it's not hard

to get the owner or CEO of a business talking about his or her accomplishments. They are usually more than willing to share valuable information with noncompetitors and to provide valuable insights into potential markets that simply are not available except from somebody who has gone through the exporting process to that market.

4. *Target market representatives.* Most countries have new business or import commissions established to help prospective sellers enter their market. As might be expected, most governments are interested in encouraging foreigners to establish plants in their country, employing local labor, and using local resources. But, at the same time, they also recognize the value of trade with other nations. The place to start for information about regulations and statistical data is the target market's trade commission in your country.

5. *International trade consultants.* These come in every shape and form, from customs expeditors to teachers of local customs. Some can take you through the whole process of exporting to a particular country, from choosing the target market to arranging for your first sales call to a prospective customer. Others are highly specialized and usually are called upon to solve specific problems. As noted earlier, your public accountant probably has an international affiliation and can likely provide some business and regulatory information on a variety of foreign markets.

6. *Trade shows.* As stated in Chapter 4, when expanding into new domestic markets was discussed, we at Premdor are great believers in trade shows as sources of information. Trade shows are the ideal place to talk to your potential customers or final users of your product or service and to get to know the competition and the type of products being sold. This is particularly valuable in a foreign market where you may know next to nothing about who is selling there or what is being produced locally. In fact, going to trade shows is one key way to narrow down target markets.

It's usually a mistake to consider participating in a trade show in a foreign country on your first trip. A great deal is involved in exhibiting the first time in another country, as well as a lot of time and expense. Only when you are convinced that you are going to make an attempt to export to that particular market should you consider exhibiting.

We can trace back one of our recent acquisitions, a door manufacturing plant in Bordeaux, France, to a contact we made several years ago at a French trade show. We had just begun exporting doors to France and were exhibiting for the first time at a trade show just outside Paris. A bilingual Frenchman showed a particular interest in our doors, to the point where he said he would quit his current job and become our sales agent in France. After a bit of investigation, we accepted his offer. Sales to France grew, as did our list of contacts.

7. *The target market itself.* In the final analysis, there is no substitute for visiting your potential market when you are preparing to export. This comes down to much more than spending a day at a trade show and flying back home that night.

Generally, the person who eventually will be most heavily involved in establishing the exporting program and who is involved from the very beginning should be the one to go on in-depth fact-finding missions to a target country. However, don't ignore some of the international facts of life when choosing particular people to head fact-finding missions.

It is not difficult to find support for your fact-finding missions to other countries. For instance, in Canada, the government of Ontario has a program that regularly sponsors trips to various areas of the United States. The two- or three-day programs are set up so that you can visit potential customers, talk to various government officials, and determine if the infrastructure of the various market suits your needs. Similar programs are available in most areas of the United States and other parts of Canada.

If you are considering a country that speaks a language you don't, you'll likely have to consider an agent familiar with the territory and your business. A simple translator may work, but chances are you'll get more out of your trip with someone at your side who is more intimate with the industry and the way of doing business in the target country. Even if language is not a problem, you should consider contacting sources in the target country. Once again, an excellent source is accountants. Chances are your accountant at home has international connections and can set up meetings with his or her counterparts in a number of countries and arrange for a much more fruitful visit than if you just step off the plane with no appointments lined up.

Evaluating the Risks and Rewards of Markets on Your Short List

Choosing one export market over another comes down to evaluating the relative risks and rewards associated with each market. Generally, the market with the least risk attached to entering and the greatest promise of *long-term* rewards gets the nod. *Long-term* reward is stressed. Premdor's only forays into foreign markets have been with the long term in mind. If you are considering a short-term export program, you likely are heading for trouble. To begin with, most such ventures are undertaken on the understanding that costs will be absolutely minimized. Therefore, you are likely to know much less about your target market than you ought to and are much more likely to encounter problems.

Risk generally involves all the potential pitfalls discussed in this section. Reward obviously involves profit, eventually, but it entails much more. For example, one of the rewards of entering a particular market is that you may gain a much greater degree of seasonal or cyclical protection than you would if you simply expanded in your domestic market. Other rewards are outlined in Chapter 6. Taking the time to properly evaluate risk and reward means that you will not make the mistake of going into an export market unprepared. One of the biggest dangers of doing that is not just that you are likely to fail—though such a failure in itself will probably be costly—but that you will give up on exporting altogether thus potentially weakening your company in the long run and missing out on the tremendous opportunities offered by exporting.

CHAPTER 8

Developing and Implementing Your Export Plan

This chapter covers the process of:

♦ Documenting specific objectives of your export strategy.

♦ Analyzing the strategy's strengths and weaknesses.

♦ Delegating responsibility within your organization for getting the export venture going.

♦ Putting the plan into action.

Lay the Groundwork in Writing

The primary purpose of developing an export plan and of *committing that plan to writing* is to create an action statement or a plan of attack. The plan keeps the company and all concerned on track throughout the process of expanding into global markets. It acts as a map of where you are going and why. And, of course, it likely will be used to gain additional financing if this is deemed necessary. These basic reasons behind planning for expansion were discussed in detail in Chapter 2.

The secondary purpose of a plan is to:

♦ Encourage commitment on the part of everyone directly involved in getting the exporting venture off the ground.

♦ Motivate them to follow through on specific decisions using criteria that are usually spelled out in the plan.

◆ Act as a benchmark against which success in meeting objectives and implementation schedules can be measured.

At the same time, a well-written and well-constructed plan can foster broader commitment to your exporting program from every area of your company. It cannot be stressed too much that everyone in your company must be committed to your expansion plans—otherwise, you will encounter internal roadblocks at some point in your expansion process. Generally, if you are committed to expansion and to exporting, anyone vital to the success of your planning should either buy into the program or possibly look at leaving the company. Expanding takes a great deal of effort, time, and money. Developing a viable, successful exporting program demands more of each than expanding domestically.

Planning an exporting program follows the same basic planning issues that are involved with any type of expansion. However, a number of additional planning issues related specifically to exporting must be included in any plan to go global. These are discussed in the following section.

Key Questions Your Plan Should Address

As has been discussed, the core of your plan should be a narrative that describes all aspects of your exporting program. Only after you have hashed out all the details of your program—including the facts, the objectives, and the potential problems to be overcome—committed them to paper, and gained agreement on them from every person to be involved with implementing and monitoring the program should you then begin to discuss and formulate numbers—that is, sales projections, pro forma financial statements, and financing requirements. If you quickly target a country, decide that you can make $10 million in sales in the first year, and put a salesperson on board an airplane, you'll likely be no further ahead at the end of the year. Numbers remain numbers unless you know exactly how and why they can be translated into sales and profit.

The following ten elements should form the heart of your detailed exporting plan. Depending on the nature of your product or service, the target market, and the nature of your competition, there could be a number of other points that should be considered.

1. Why Are You Developing an Export Program?

This is the question you should have answered as you read Chapter 6. Your reasons should be committed to paper and should introduce your formal written plan. Exporting may be your first step in expanding outside your domestic market. If your exporting foray into the target market is successful, you may consider establishing a plant or a stronger presence in that market. Or you may want to expand your physical operations, so you have targeted foreign markets in which to sell the increased number of goods you'll be able to produce. Or you are looking to decrease seasonal or cyclical risk by expanding globally. Or you may have saturated your domestic market, and you have no choice but to turn to foreign markets.

Whatever your reasons, they should be logically constructed and communicated to everyone who will be involved in the exporting program.

2. What Market Do You Plan to Enter and Why?

This is the question that you have answered as you conducted your fact-finding mission. You looked at all the pros and cons of several markets, performed a risk-reward analysis, and decided on one or perhaps several target markets. Your reasons for choosing the particular market should be outlined in your written plan, and the various pros and cons, that is, the points that went into your risk-reward analysis, should be highlighted.

Documenting this part of the decision-making process in your plan can pay dividends in the future. If things don't work out, you can turn back to your analysis to see where you may have made mistakes. Or if things work out extremely well, you have a blueprint for approaching your next target market. It also can be used to explain to newcomers to the exporting program why you have chosen a particular market and why exporting to that market is expected to benefit the company more than exporting to any of dozens of other markets.

3. What Products Will You Take to the Target Market?

This question generally should have been answered as you conducted your research and fact-finding. Much of your research involved determining demand for your product, competing products, consumer preferences, and a host of other related information. First, you should have good reasons why one of several products that you make is the one you are planning to export. Generally, it's safest to export the product that has the strongest sales at home and generates the most profit. If there is demand for it domestically, it is reasonable to expect that there will be demand for it in other parts of the world. This is not always the case, of course. You may have a sideline product that has very little competition in a particular foreign market. Or your major product may have so much competition that you simply can't enter that market and compete on price. Or the target country may have little use for your major line.

Second, you should know whether you will have to modify your product in any way and whether new packaging and labeling will be needed. What kind of modifications will have to be made to your sales and promotional material and your catalogues? Will any special packaging arrangements have to be made for shipping? Should your product be presented to consumers a little differently on the shelves? Will your product react a little differently in a new climate?

Finally, assuming relatively quick success selling one product into your target market, you should have some idea of how you are going to meet demand. You also should be thinking of how you are going to exploit your initial success by selling different product lines into your target market. In fact, your satisfied customers may be the first to ask whether you have anything else as good to sell.

4. How Do You Plan to Enter the Market?

Again, you should have done your research during the fact-finding stage to determine how you are going to ship and sell in the target market. One of the most common mistakes novice exporters make is not researching thoroughly exactly how their products are going to get from the domestic factory into the foreign consumers' hands. Demand can be strong and competition weak, but if you can't deliver your product effectively, you won't achieve success.

It's unlikely that you will begin by selling your products directly to retail outlets. In most instances, you will be selling to wholesalers or distributors. You may use your own salespeople or you may use an agent who is familiar with that foreign market.

Much of your success depends on how well you choose your distributor or agent. Most distributors are willing to take on new product lines if no risk is involved. However, getting a distributor to take on your product does not necessarily mean that he or she will actively sell it or take as much care and interest in promoting it as you would if you were on site in the foreign market. You also have to take care assigning distribution rights. If rights go to one distributor for the entire country, you have put all your eggs in one basket, and your success will depend on that distributor's ability to sell your product. Selling to many distributors in different areas can be more expensive than selling to one. But since you have not entered into long-term agreements, you have the option of searching out new distributors until you have lined up the team you want.

It is important to take your time when choosing a distributor and to choose the best distributor for each of your foreign markets. In many industries, going with the wrong distributor in a particular market—one who fails to push your product hard enough, for example—can stop your export venture dead in its tracks.

More and more companies with export programs are developing alliances with companies in the foreign market. Typically, you look for a company producing a complementary product in the foreign market. That company sells and distributes your product, and you take on the responsibility of distributing and selling that company's product in your domestic market. You both have a vested interest in each other's success, so you both have a much better chance of achieving success in each other's market. Such alliances can go a long way to helping you understand your export market and, thus, do a better job selling in it. And they can help you understand your foreign competitors, which, in turn, helps you protect your markets at home.

5. What Kind of Obstacles Are You Likely to Encounter?

No exporting program goes smoothly. You are entering unfamiliar territory and are bound to make mistakes, read the signs incorrectly, or overlook an area that needs to be researched. There's no substitute for hands-on experience and, eventually, there's no other way to learn about exporting than by just doing it.

Proper research will at least alert you to the types of roadblocks you may encounter. And proper research also should allow you to deal with most of these roadblocks before you hit them head-on or they shut down your export program entirely. A review of Chapter 2 will indicate the types of obstacles that you will have to address in your export plan.

One common obstacle is the fact that every company planning to export will have to jump numerous regulatory hurdles, from new tax and customs regimes to consumer and environmental protection legislation to product standards regulations. The learning curve is different from country to country.

A t Premdor, we have to file tax and various information returns in every state in the United States and every province in Canada in which we have plants or offices. And, of course, we have to file federal tax returns in both countries. We also have to file returns and observe various reporting requirements in ten other countries. At the same time, we have to keep up-to-date on all ongoing regulatory issues. Transferring goods to one country and money out of that country usually involves duties or tariffs, commodity taxes, and withholding taxes. It is extremely complicated, but we have no choice but to stay on top of it on a daily basis. While we certainly use external professional help every so often for specific complex issues, we try to handle as much as possible ourselves. We decided this very early on in our expansion planning, and thus assigned responsibility for such matters to our chief financial officer and one of our vice presidents who was formerly a partner at a law firm.

---

6. Who Is Going to Quarterback Your Exporting Effort?

While the CEO or owner of the business is likely to be the moving force behind an exporting program, someone should be appointed to take responsibility for the push into the target market. You cannot have someone handling domestic sales and, at the same time, trying to develop export opportunities. Developing your export market is a full-time job. The person chosen should be responsible for all research and fact-finding, and he or she should produce the exporting plan.

The quarterback also should know exactly what resources will be available to pursue the program. As discussed earlier, he or she should have confidence that a certain amount of money is available to pursue various phases of the program and that the right personnel, who must be committed to the export program, will be available when and where they are needed.

However, your quarterback may not be the right person to pursue the plan inside the foreign market. Language, for instance, may be a problem. And as much as possible, you should attempt to have local people in that market involved in all aspects of your operation. Your research should tell you whether you should hire an agent in the market to sell your product or use one of your own people. Still, you need that one person to take charge, implement the plan, assess results, and report back to head office. If you decide to hire a foreign manager who understands the local market and its customers, you will have to be prepared to give him or her a fair degree of latitude to operate. At the same time, however, you also will have to set up good controls and internal reporting systems to maintain accountability, particularly financial accountability.

7. What Is Your Timing?

You won't be able to establish a presence in your export market overnight. In fact, it may take one or two years from the time you begin your research to the time you make your first sale. You aren't going to be welcomed with open arms in a competitive market. And even in a market where the competition is not particularly strong, it still may take months to determine the best initial approach to securing sales.

The assumption has been made that you are expanding into exporting for the long term. You intend for your export markets to become a profitable cornerstone of your business. Therefore you have to give the whole process the time it needs and deserves. It usually takes at least six months to become relatively familiar with an unfamiliar market and to get to know what consumers want, how business is done, and how to function under the regulatory regime. You will then need another six months to determine how to price your product or service, to whom you are going to sell it, and how you will get it to market. Again, think of how you expanded your business domestically. It didn't happen overnight; it was a continual learning process. Don't make the mistake of thinking that your success at home will translate directly to a foreign market. If you attempt to compress your preparation for going global into a month or two, you are very likely not doing a thorough job on any aspect of the entire process. And that's a recipe for failure.

8. How Is Your Exporting Effort Being Financed?

When you are entering a new market, it's important to bear in mind that you are making a capital investment. You are putting a fair amount of money into the venture up front and hoping for a return over time. We have all heard of extraordinary exporting stories—one sales call, little preparation, and million dollar markets over night. These cases are the exception, and even they are often only one-shot deals after which the company never sees any follow-up sales, usually because it couldn't follow up on any of its initial promises. The more realistic scenario is that you will have to invest a significant amount of money to develop and execute your export plan—and you will to have to be patient for a return on that money.

Ideally, you should try to finance your exporting effort internally. The comments made on financing expansion in Chapter 2 apply to export financing. All expansion involves risk. It's better to risk your own money than the bank's money. If success isn't forthcoming, at least you have your domestic business to fall back on with no huge debt load hanging over your operations.

If you need a significant amount of financing, you can try the normal avenues—the banks and other lenders—and they will likely be as responsive as they are to financing your domestic expansion. Bear in mind that when you go global, lenders will likely want to keep a closer eye on your operations, and you very likely won't be able to go to them for day-to-day operating financing for receivables and inventory. But, if you can insure or guarantee your receivables, or you can sell by letters of credit, your bank will usually be amenable to financing.

There are, however, many other financing alternatives. Your federal, state, provincial, or even municipal government has programs available that can help in every area of financing your exporting program, from loans or grants to cover the cost of fact-finding missions and visits to target markets, to investment in new plant or equipment to service an export market, to loans and guarantees on your foreign receivables.

Don't neglect to analyze the impact of your export venture on your day-to-day financial situation. How will the new program affect your cash flow, receivables, balance sheet, inventory, capacity, and so on?

9. What Are the Goals of Your Exporting Program?

Only at this stage should you start generating some numbers. This is exactly the same exercise that you would go through with any other type of expansion. First you develop a narrative that outlines your goals, how you plan to achieve them, and why you will be able to achieve success, and only after everyone has agreed on the narrative do you begin attaching numbers and projections to those goals.

However, when you are developing exporting numbers, it pays to be particularly conservative. No matter how much research you have done, you won't know your target market as well as your domestic market and, therefore, it is much more likely that a few curves will be thrown your way as you implement your program. It is especially important to be conservative if the banks are making loans or outside investors are putting up money that is connected with your exporting venture.

Your goals may not be focused strictly on profitability. For instance:

♦ Your primary goal may be to maintain a certain level of production in your plant, no matter what the domestic environment, in order to protect your skilled workforce. Therefore, you will be inclined to accept a lower than normal level of profitability from your export markets.

♦ Or, your goal may be to lower your domestic costs by increasing the amount of product you produce and thereby lowering overheads. This allows you to compete more effectively at home. In this case, again, you may not be primarily concerned with your exports generating high levels of profit.

Such goals should be carefully spelled out in your plan, but no one should get the idea that exports are to continually be a loss leader. You must always take care to avoid anti-dumping rules, which discourage foreign companies from undercutting domestic pricing just to take market share.

10. How Do You Plan to Keep Score?

Obviously, part of your scorekeeping has to do with measuring financial performance against goals that you have established. You also should consider implementing progress reports on your exporting program. For example, you may discover that developing export markets is a great learning experience that not only strengthens your company but also benefits everyone involved. Specifically, you may learn new methods of production and new sales strategies. Your reporting and financial systems may undergo changes for the better as a direct result of having to adapt to doing business in another country. And your people may grow immensely as they have to deal with the many challenges posed by doing business in another culture. These types of advances should be set out periodically and communicated to everyone in your organization. And don't neglect to highlight the setbacks and disappointments. We have always learned from our mistakes. Make sure that your people get the same opportunity.

By taking all of these questions into account and integrating their answers with the information gained through your research and fact-finding efforts, you will be able to produce your export plan. A preliminary outline for that plan might look like the one shown in Figure 8-1.

How Will You Track Your Progress?

Monitoring your exporting venture involves the same type of measures and scrutiny that you apply to the rest of your business every day. However, when it comes to exporting, you will want to intensify application of those measures and that scrutiny, at least in the early stages. It's a new direction for your company, and it's more likely to go offtrack at some point. And there are a few sensitive spots in any export program that must be observed closely on a day-to-day basis.

Figure 8-1. **Preliminary outline for an export plan.**

Section I. Executive Summary

Section II. Narrative
♦ Reasons company should export.
♦ Market targeted.
♦ Reasons for selecting target market.
♦ Product(s) to be exported.
♦ Short-term/long-term market outlook.

Section III. Key Events/Assumptions
♦ Key industry indicators in target market and forecasts for upward/downward trends; include specific numbers.
♦ Effect of these trends on demand for your product.
♦ Predicted level of activity in target market compared to that of current domestic market.
♦ Key economic and/or political factors, if any, that will affect (positively or negatively) activity in your market.

Section IV. Major Market Segments and Opportunities/Market Analysis
♦ Segmentation of the target market and relative importance of each segment to your business. For each segment, include information on the following:
  ◊ Size of segment; proportion of the total market.
  ◊ Type of customer this segment serves—final user? Wholesaler? Retailer?
  ◊ What are channels of distribution within this segment?
  ◊ What products are sold to this segment? Are products sold in finished/semifinished state? What proportion of products sold are customized? Do all competitors use same specifications?
  ◊ What is competitors' pricing and quality? How does it compare to yours?
  ◊ What proportion of the total market for your type of goods does this segment represent?
  ◊ Number of major competitors; market share of each.
♦ Current opportunities.

Continued on next page

Figure 8-1. *(continued)*

♦ Problems/challenges involved in serving each segment; include transportation, distribution, and possible product/packaging modifications.

♦ Opportunities to be evaluated and developed as appropriate during the year.

Section V. Internal Resources and Organization

♦ Who makes up the export team?

♦ Internal organization of sales and marketing teams.

  ◇ Will local manager be needed in export market?

  ◇ Will new sales representatives need to be hired?

  ◇ Will you use distributors?

♦ Operational capacity.

  ◇ What resources will be dedicated to the export venture?

Section VI. This Year's Plan—Priorities/Timetable

♦ Organizational issues.

  ◇ Delegate regular responsibilities of export team members to other staff and get them up to speed.

  ◇ If needed, commence search for local manager immediately; when should local manager be in place?

  ◇ If needed, hire additional sales representatives; when should they be in place?

♦ Sales and marketing issues.

  ◇ Begin to develop relationships with distributors.

  ◇ Have distribution agreements in place by what date?

♦ Implementation—what is the timetable for the launch?

♦ Monitoring.

  ◇ Monitor financial information daily.

  ◇ Monitor sales results weekly.

  ◇ Arrange for monthly progress report.

  ◇ Perform operational and management review quarterly.

Section VII. Financial Highlights

♦ Pro forma financial statements.

♦ Sales projections.

♦ Financing requirements.

The five main areas you will need to monitor to ensure your success are:

1. Product quality.

2. Pricing.

3. Receivables.

4. Currency fluctuations.

5. Sales and cost of sales.

Ensuring Product Quality

For most types of exports, it's almost impossible to take back defective product. It's simply not economical to repack, ship home, repair, and ship back to the foreign customer product that should have gone out in good order in the first place. Yet, untold numbers of companies learn this lesson the hard way. Whether because of eagerness to get the order out, lack of sufficient quality control or supervision in domestic operations, or miscommunication, shipments go out with problems that come back to haunt exporters. Once you have some experience in foreign markets and have had time to observe exporters in all industries, not just your own, it's not difficult to begin to form a picture in your mind. That picture is of warehouse after warehouse around the world filled with defective products that manufacturers decided to abandon or sell at a fraction of cost rather than pay to ship home. Premdor has paid this price more than once. A certain amount of defective product is unavoidable, especially if you are producing thousands of units a day, but improving your quality control is vital if you want to pursue export markets seriously.

We know of a shelving company that shipped the wrong type of screw with a container load of shelving that had to be assembled by the customer on the premises. If the shelving had been shipped to a customer 100 miles down the road, the proper screws could have been delivered a few hours after the problem was discovered. If the shelves have been shipped half way around the world, you have a much more serious problem, especially if your customers can't find those screws locally. Shipping the proper ones by air may take two days, which the customer may or may not be able to live with, but the cost may wipe out any profit on the sale.

It is also true that your new international customers will not appreciate any fall down in the quality of your product or service. Your product is likely one of many similar products manufactured around the world. Competition has improved quality over the last decade or two, and no one can afford to ship goods that are less than first rate. Your domestic customers may be willing to accept a certain level of problems, primarily because you are selling your service as well as your product. You are able to solve their problems quickly and efficiently. This won't be the case if you are selling overseas. Remember that the first thing your new customers will see is the quality of your product. Only after they have become customers for a period of time will they come to appreciate your service.

Ensuring or improving the quality of your products might mean testing them more vigorously before they go out the door. Paying attention to product quality might also mean randomly pulling product from finished goods inventory and giving it an intensive once-over. Is the labeling legible? Are the screws that are supposed to be included in the packaging included? Are they the correct screws? If your product has a paint finish, is the finish flawless or are there tiny scratches or chips?

When it is practical—for example, if you export expensive, high-tech equipment—another way of ensuring product quality is to maintain a computerized record of each unit exported. If a customer calls from half way around the world, the history of the unit, such as whether certain parts were replaced during testing, will be immediately accessible. Not only will this allow you to provide good customer service, it also will allow you to track performance of your units in real work situations and perhaps alert you to potential weak spots in design or production.

Remember that making the effort to monitor the quality of the goods you export will also pay dividends at home. It will help you make your products better, and that should help you increase sales and/or profit margins in your domestic markets.

Monitoring Pricing

It goes without saying that you want to price competitively. You certainly don't want to operate at a loss, but you don't want to price yourself out of the market either.

If you enter a foreign market with prices that are too low, you may actually deter potential customers who will doubt the quality of your goods.

Remember, too, that it is much more difficult to raise prices if you start off too low. Your potential or former customers will wonder why you couldn't get it right the first time. They certainly will object to higher prices if they have become used to the lower prices and are basing their profit forecasts on these lower prices. And you will have given the customers you have fought hard to acquire an excuse to go over to the competition.

If you are using a distributor or agent in your export market, you will have to figure this person's fee into your pricing. If the distributor's fee or markup on your product is too high, you may not be as competitive as you could be and you could develop an image of being pricey, which may discourage potential customers and repeat sales. When you set your pricing, also consider the impact of exchange rates (see the following section on currency fluctuations).

Once you think you have your pricing right, keeping it right is an ongoing challenge. Suppose you are introducing a new or different product into the export market that can be priced a little higher or lower than competing products because of the lack of direct similarities. Because your goods are not strictly comparable to those currently sold on the market, you will have to monitor your pricing and sales on a regular, even daily, basis. In order to do so, you must have both the financial reporting systems and analytical capabilities to turn data into meaningful information. As discussed in Chapter 2, these resources are central to maintaining control over your operations and your expansion.

You also should assess the competitiveness of your pricing through monthly reports from your distributors or agents. But don't rely entirely on them. Nothing can replace direct feedback from your overseas customers. So make a point of always keeping in touch and gathering information from them, too.

In the final analysis, your pricing must be competitive in your export market. But you can't rely on pricing alone for success. You also will have to compete on the basis of your ability to fill orders and deliver them on time, as well as on your product quality and customer service.

Collecting Receivables

If you can't collect from your new customers, you can't make a profit. Collecting from foreign customers is usually more difficult than collecting from domestic customers, primarily because you are not as familiar with business customs in the foreign country. It's Premdor's experience that we get paid if we do proper credit checks and focus our efforts on long-term customer relationships. If customers want to buy from you again, they will always pay for the previous shipment. Companies looking for a quick hit in the first export market that presents itself or to take advantage of a temporary situation are usually the ones that get burned. The one big sale is everything, not a longer-term relationship. Such exporters haven't done their research, and their customers know it. Some of their customers may also feel that if they are likely never to see the exporter again, there is no point in paying promptly or perhaps even paying at all. After all, the costs involved in pursuing delinquent accounts from outside the country is usually prohibitively high, and taking back product once it has been shipped is usually extremely difficult.

If you can sell by letters of credit, secure payment in advance, or have your receivables insured or guaranteed, collecting receivables does not present much of a problem. Extra costs for you or for your customers are involved using any other method. Direct payment by check is the method that promotes the best kind of seller-buyer relations.

Accounts receivable are treated differently in each country, so it is important that you understand the methods of doing business in the foreign markets you enter. Factoring and credit insurance (as discussed in Chapter 7) are very common in some countries. Also, salespeople can play an important role in helping monitor receivables by staying close to customers. But the surest way to avoid problems with tracking receivables is to follow one basic rule: "Don't ship if you haven't been paid."

Monitoring Currency Fluctuations

It's impossible, or extremely costly, to guard against every potential currency surprise. But it is easy to ensure that your domestic costs of producing and shipping your product match what you eventually receive in foreign currency from the buyer. You simply buy foreign futures contracts in that currency and price accordingly. Yes, there is a cost involved, but what you are buying is certainty. You know that the amount you eventually receive for product made and shipped several months ago will cover your costs and produce the kind of profit you want.

Monitoring and allowing for currency fluctuations is an essential part of exporting. You cannot export successfully over the longer term without taking the costs of anticipated and unanticipated currency fluctuations into account. No currency in the world remains static or in lock step with your domestic currency for long.

Ideally, you should have someone on staff who specifically takes care of and monitors foreign currency matters. It's not necessary for that person to make complex foreign currency decisions, but the person should at least be aware of possible problems and be able to take action in concert with financial professionals.

Tracking Sales and Cost of Sales

How you monitor your export sales depends on the nature of your product, the assumptions you have made about how quickly you will penetrate the foreign market, the level of competition, and competitors' reactions to you, among other things. In fact, you probably will be continually revising your sales forecasts as you become more familiar with the market. Of course, at the same time, you must monitor prices to ensure that you remain competitive and keep on the profit track that you have decided is acceptable. And you must continually monitor your cost of sales, much the same as you do for domestic sales. However, you should pay particular attention to all the added costs that producing for and shipping to unfamiliar markets entail to ensure that these are not getting out of hand and that they are indeed being accounted for in the pricing of your product or service.

One mistake some exporters make is to not differentiate between the cost of developing an export market and the cost of selling to that market. The former is an investment, the latter simply your cost of doing business in the foreign market. The cost of getting ready to make your first sale is not the same as the cost involved in making that and subsequent sales. The investment made in developing an export market is long-term and strategic and should be thought of in the same way as writing off, over time, the cost of acquiring a piece of machinery.

When you want to start making a profit on your exports depends on the nature of your product, the competition, your company, and your investors. Some want a profit to show up in the first year, although they are willing to write the investment portion off over two or three years. Other organizations are willing to wait five years for profitable export operations. No matter which camp you fall into, don't make the mistake of including those up-front investment costs in with the cost of selling your product. If it costs $1 million to target a market, do your research, and set up the proper structure in your company to handle your exporting program, you can't add that $1 million on to the cost of your first shipment of product. If you do, obviously your pricing will be completely off base and you probably won't be able to compete very successfully in your new market.

The development costs should be factored into your pricing, but they must be factored in on a rational basis that does not skew your longer-term pricing structure. You ought to decide up front the period over which you want to apportion those development costs to sales. For example, if you expect to be in a profitable position in two years and reach some level of stability in five years, you might opt to apportion those costs over the five-year period. If you add those costs into your first year or two of exporting, your results will suffer. You may have a perfectly viable exporting program under way, but the numbers are going to say that you are losing too much money and should perhaps get out of that particular market.

Implementing Your Plan

Once you have targeted an export market, done the necessary research and fact-finding, developed and written out a comprehensive export plan, and set up the appropriate monitoring systems, implementation of your plan is a relatively easy last step—and one for which you are completely prepared. The most important point to bear in mind at this stage is that you must have the right people on board to carry out a successful implementation. If you will be selling directly in the foreign market, you must decide whether it will be more effective to have your own people selling or to hire someone in the foreign market. You need a support staff at home to deal with the new market and all the curves it will throw at you over the first year or two. It is critical that your support staff be prepared to deal with unusual problems that they have never met before. They must be flexible and accommodating. Premdor realized early on that our way was not the only way. Whether it is a matter of the need for product modifications or adapting to different methods of distribution, we found that each market has its own demands. Your ability to be flexible will be a great strength in exporting.

Ideally, your advance preparation, including reading this book, has shortened the export learning curve or made it much less steep. Still, no matter how much research you conduct or planning you undertake, you will encounter a learning curve as you expand into export markets. Premdor's experience has been that the more you plan, the easier it is to enter a new market successfully. It probably is possible to overplan and overspend on planning, but you won't regret the results. Of course, there always comes a time when you have to get out there and start selling and shipping. But that doesn't mean that your learning is suddenly over with. It probably will take several years to understand all the nuances of doing business profitably in a foreign country. Some businesses don't take the time to learn and retreat sooner or later. Others learn quickly and achieve a level of success that is the envy of their competitors and others looking at the same market. These are the businesses that you want to learn from.

PART FOUR

Expanding for Your Own Good

CHAPTER 9

Expansion as a Process of Continuous Improvement

This chapter outlines:

♦ How expansion positions your company for the 1990s.

♦ Why expansion involves risk.

♦ How you can manage that risk.

The benefits of expanding your business are many: increased profitability, increased and better use of capacity, diversification that offers protection against slumps in particular markets or product lines, more effective use of resources, better access to raw materials and personnel—the list goes on. Perhaps most important, expanding means that you are changing. And if your expansion program is to be successful, any changes you make have to, by definition, be for the better. As mentioned in Chapter 1, any business that stands still in the 1990s is courting disaster. The new realities of the marketplace demand that you adapt to a rapidly changing business environment.

Expanding successfully will have a positive impact on your business in a number of other ways. This can be summed up succinctly: Tough conditions teach you to be tough on yourself, and new horizons open up new and better ways of approaching your business. Perhaps the most significant factor responsible for putting businesses on the long slide downward into unprofitability is complacency—taking your customer base, your product or service, and the way you've always done things for granted. Your customers may have gotten into the same rut also, buying and using your product, paying the price, but never really looking at it or at competing products. Eventually they do, however, and, if they find your product or any other aspect of your business lacking, they are just as likely to switch suppliers as talk to you about your problems.

Developing and putting into action an expansion program virtually guarantees that you will be shaken out of any complacency that may have set in. If you are to expand successfully, you have to reexamine every facet of your organization. And once you set your expansion plans in motion, customers, competition, and a variety of market forces will drive you to improve any number of aspects of your business, from product design to packaging, from the accounting system to the way you serve customers. Dealing in an expanded marketplace will make you think more carefully and constructively about everything you and your business do. In other words, growth is good for the health of your business. Companies that conduct a successful expansion program position themselves to expand successfully again and to compete more successfully in domestic and foreign markets.

Evaluate Your Product or Service Through Your Customers' Eyes

When you sell to new customers outside your established market, whether they are in new domestic markets or foreign markets, they aren't likely to blindly accept your product or service the way your current customers do. These new customers will examine your product or service carefully, take it apart and put it back together, test it thoroughly to make sure it stands up to their demands, and then assess whether or not they are getting value for their money. And they are not going to stop there. They will tell you everything they have found out about your product or service and let you know of their complaints or suggestions for improvement—how to make it more safe or more convenient to use, how to make it less expensively, why certain features are not all that useful, what other features they would like to see, what defects they found in the packaging, and so on. They will let you know how your quality control measures up to your competitors' and what you might think about doing to improve service.

New customers are going to be curious about your product or service. You've got to become just as curious if you want to keep them as customers. You've got to listen to what they have to say. If they find problems, you've got to fix them. Usually, they will find problems that you didn't realize you had. And this is always good for the health of your business. It's the rare company that is actually the best in the world at what it does and is always the leader. But most companies can get close to that position if they look at their products, and every aspect of their business for that matter, through the eyes of their toughest customer. In fact, developing new customers through expanding gives you the perfect opportunity to invite comments, criticism, and suggestions.

Review Production Processes

Learning of problems with your product often leads to discovering problems in your production process. If your current customers are happy, you may have never bothered to investigate different, more efficient, cost-effective ways of making your product. Through dealing with new, more critical customers, you may discover that the problems they uncover are a result of doing things the way they have always been done. Doing things differently could be as fundamental and far-reaching as introducing computerized production, or could be as simple as rescheduling the order in which various functions are performed. The key is that selling to new customers as a result of your expansion program makes you look at this side of your business differently and more critically.

Just as importantly, you will be able to tap into the accumulated knowledge of your new, larger customer base. Many may have operations that are similar to yours and will be willing to share information on increasing productivity or developing new methods of manufacturing.

New customers also may allow you to tap into new sources of supplies and raw materials. This is another aspect of complacency that creeps up on many producers. They have used the same suppliers for years and, after a while, stopped questioning the quality and price of materials they buy. The supplier's service is good and profitability does not appear to have been affected, so alternatives have never been investigated. New customers usually have new ways of doing things, and that includes using different suppliers. Again, they will be more than happy to introduce you to these suppliers. It's in their best interest, because if you can buy goods more cheaply or of better quality, you will end up supplying your new customers with a better, less expensive product. New customers also underline the fact that life is a two-way street. Through dealing in new markets, you may be introduced to new products that you can bring back to your existing markets.

Consider New Distribution Methods

Just because you have always done it one way, doesn't mean that it's the only way. If you now ship products as far as 300 miles, you can't assume that the same methods you use will be suitable if you begin shipping 3,000 miles or offshore. If you are developing new markets or exporting, transportation and distribution become a larger component of cost. If your program is successful, you will undoubtedly have researched various transportation and distribution alternatives. In this search, you will likely come across new methods or opportunities that may have an application in your domestic market.

And again, you will likely learn from your new customers, or be forced to learn. More and more companies are relying on electronic data interchange (EDI) systems for ordering and controlling inventory. To develop new customers in your new target market, perhaps you had to upgrade your computer system and develop a new way to distribute your products quickly and efficiently. What you learn and implement to satisfy your new customer base you can also use on behalf of your existing customers. In fact, your new, more efficient distribution system may be the key to keeping your current customers and winning new ones domestically.

Research New Approaches to Marketing

To enter a new market, you probably had to research how competitors marketed their products, what kind of advertising they used, how important a component service was to their whole package, and what your potential customers were accustomed to and looking for in the marketing area. This exposure to a much broader range of competing products and new, more critical customers is valuable information that you can put to work in your current markets, whether to solidify sales or expand your customer base. They may do things differently in Denver, but they also may do them better. It's this type of knowledge that is so valuable and that you can use for your benefit.

At Premdor, we are particularly interested in trade shows. And in the building products industry, there are plenty of them all over the world, all the time. These are one of the main sources of our information. We get an up-close look at the competition's products, but just as importantly, we get to look at their marketing and sales effort first hand and compare it to our own efforts. Trade shows are a source for ideas. Premdor has remained competitive over the last ten years, through good times and bad, and through virtually nonstop expansion, because we are always looking for new ideas. As far as we are concerned, the knowledge bank is never full. We have always got something to learn. Every new customer or competitor has something to teach us, and we actively search it out.

Look for New Product or Market Opportunities

Developing new customers, particularly in new locales, typically opens your eyes to what is needed in the new market. Because a particular area is saturated at home, you may have assumed that it is saturated elsewhere, so you have abandoned plans to produce or sell that particular product. In most cases, that turns out to be a bad assumption. No markets are exactly the same. That's one thing you will discover as you expand. And the more you look, the more opportunities you will discover. These may come from your new customers saying they don't have a reliable supply of widgets. Or you may discover that nobody is showing gizmos at the biggest and best trade show in your new market. As you develop new customers in your new market, it may turn out to be very simple to add widgets or gizmos to your product line.

At the same time, keeping your eyes open in your new markets should cause you to open them a little wider in your current market. Perhaps you have been approaching the sale of gizmos or widgets the wrong way. You might be able to package them with a complementary product and achieve success. Or you might be able to enter into an alliance with a distributor and make inroads in your current market. Once again, the important point to bear in mind is that you have learned something in your expansion market, and this knowledge can be taken home and applied successfully.

Exposing yourself to your new markets also exposes you to more products. Perhaps your new customers are using such products or you see them at a trade show you have never before attended. These products may be new or may never have made their way into your existing market. Whatever the case, they present an opportunity that you would not have known about unless you were expanding.

Your new customers also may reveal new market opportunities. For instance, you might be making sales to a certain type of company in your new market. With a little digging, you may discover similar companies that have the same needs and would be likely sales targets. If pursued, these opportunities may open up further sales in these other markets.

Once again, this tack could be pursued in your existing markets— many companies have not made the most of the customers they do have. It is also likely that the larger customer base that results from expansion may lead to further sales in your current territory. If much of your sales come from referrals and networking, it stands to reason that the more customers you have, the more referrals you should get.

Reassess Your Financial Base

If tough customers have made you thoroughly reexamine your products and production, they also will make you look much more closely at your bottom line. This will be especially true if you are up against much stiffer competition in the new market than you currently encounter. To remain competitive in any market, you either must continually reduce costs or improve the quality of your product. You can't stand still and simply raise prices to offset increasing costs.

Being exposed to new markets, new competition, and new customers will reveal the strengths and weaknesses of your financial base. Developing a new market, exporting, or acquiring a company require financial resources. Expanding successfully means that you have the resources in place to handle many situations.

Most companies will experience exactly this type of financial pressure at home whether they expand or not. Again the watchword is change. Your market is changing and your customers are changing. You have to change with them. And this requires financing. If you have undertaken the type of financial planning for expansion outlined earlier in the book, and are aware of your capabilities for financing a major expansion, you should be well-prepared to plan for and meet the financial challenges of change in your current market.

Upgrade Your Accounting Systems

The importance of accurate and timely reporting systems has been stressed throughout the book. You simply cannot make informed, quality decisions without the right kind of information at your fingertips. Any type of expansion forces most companies to look for and develop types of information that they were not producing in the past. Expansion also forces them to produce information more regularly and on a more timely basis. If you are investing several million dollars in an acquisition, for instance, you want to know how the purchase is working out, often on a daily basis. Or if a new customer demands some price concession, you want to know exactly how this affects your profit on the sale. For most companies, this means an upgrade to their accounting system, making it more sophisticated and capable of producing exactly the kind of information that is necessary to the expansion program.

In virtually all cases, this type of upgrading will benefit your current business. It stands to reason that if you need this type of information for your expansion program, your current business should also benefit. For example, once a company begins to look at different measures of profitability and productivity, it often discovers defects in its current or domestic business. While bottom line profit may be acceptable, the company may discover that its worker productivity is not up to the standards being set by the competition in its new markets. This signals that the company could be heading for rough times in its existing markets since it is probably just a matter of time before that same competition casts an eye towards those markets.

However, if you have developed a system for providing more, better, and more timely information, this is the best kind of defense you can develop against new competition, assuming of course that you act on this information. In the long run, having this type of information readily available means that you can lower costs, lower prices if necessary, and strengthen your position in your current and your new markets.

Be Aware of Currency Fluctuations

One of the reasons you decided to expand was undoubtedly to diversify your operations so that a downturn in one market or in one product line would not have such a severe impact on your bottom line. If you have decided to export or set up operations in a foreign country, you also will have learned the value of hedging against foreign currency fluctuations.

The hedging techniques that you use to control revenues can also be used to control costs. More and more companies are sourcing a variety of materials from other countries. It is vital that you know what the cost will be in your own currency for purposes of pricing your products or services, even though you may have committed to buy those materials some months earlier. Currency hedges smooth out fluctuations in cost. Thus, exporting will help with importing.

Gain Employees' Commitment to Your Expansion Plan

It's difficult to expand successfully unless you have a committed, skilled workforce that is eager to embrace the expansion program. Not all workforces are automatically this committed. You generally have to work to encourage them and foster the attitude that is necessary to make your expansion plan work. Of course, once your workforce is completely dedicated to your expansion vision, the benefits on the existing side of your business soon become apparent. Relations among employee groups and employees and management typically improve. Workers become more productive because they are being challenged and properly rewarded.

The question asked by most CEOs or business owners after such an exercise is "why didn't we pay more attention to human resources long ago?" Again the reason is complacency. If you don't have obvious problems with your workforce, why bother working at improving it if profitability seems to be adequate? The answer is change. Your business and your industry will change. If you don't change for the better at the same time, you are putting your business in jeopardy. Even thinking about expanding gives you the impetus to look at your business more critically and determine where changes could be, or have to be, made.

Evaluate Your Management Team and Structure

With any type of expansion, you must review the abilities and capabilities of your management team before you begin to make serious plans. As noted earlier, the team has to be committed, motivated, and energetic. During my ten years at Premdor working with our management team, I've discovered that there is no substitute for intelligence, curiosity, and creativity. The best kind of management team consists of genuinely bright people at the peak of their skills. They do not necessarily have to be experienced in particular aspects of expansion; this will come in quick order as they develop and implement the expansion plan. But they must be extremely capable. If you have decided to follow a long-term expansion program, as Premdor has, you want the best team members you can find. Some people look on expansion as an endless series of problems looking for solutions. They are at least half right. You need the kind of people on your management team who relish problem solving, who look at situations and figure out better ways to handle things, who are not afraid to test out new methods of dealing with problems, and who are always searching out new opportunities and new challenges for themselves and for the company.

One of the most critical aspects of your expansion management team is their outlook. You all have to be on the same schedule or you will encounter problems. For example, if some members of your team are looking forward one, two, or three years, but you have a much longer-term, ten-year horizon in mind, you are going to be out of sync. You will want to do things that may only pay off in ten years, but some members of your team will resist these kind of actions as not paying off quickly enough. In the final analysis, it is not the age of your management team that is important but their attitude and commitment to the company and its objectives.

As you implement more and more of your expansion plan, the structure of your management team becomes more critical. Growing from 100 to 1,000 employees at one location with one product obviously will mean changes in management structure. But these changes may be very different if you grow from one to ten locations with 100 employees at each location. And a different structure may be necessary if you develop ten new product lines to go along with those new locations. As the structure of your management team evolves over time, chances are your existing business will benefit. In most cases, new people will be added who focus on particular aspects of your complete business. This type of focused expertise usually produces positive results in the area and for the business as a whole.

Expand Your Knowledge Base

It should go without saying that the more you're exposed to, the more you learn. If you have assembled the right kind of management team and fostered the right kind of attitude in your workforce, this certainly will be the case. And it will show in every aspect of your business. A great number of things learned during the whole expansion process can be applied to other aspects of your business to everyone's benefit. Many of these things are the type that just can't be learned if you stick to your existing business. Companies that embrace change, think in terms of expansion, and are constantly striving for improvement are generally longer-lived and more profitable than other companies. And they are certainly better, more enjoyable places to work.

As your company's knowledge base is expanding, however, you may run into the "how do you keep them down on the farm after they've seen Paris" dilemma. By expanding, you will likely improve the skills of virtually everybody working for the company. As a consequence, your employees are more employable and will be sought after by the competition or other employers. Your job is to keep together the team that is making your expansion so successful. Generally, you do this by giving them more of what you have been providing—more education, more special training, added responsibility, more challenges, and more rewards in the forms of remuneration, profit sharing, perks, or even time off. Study after study has shown that motivated, challenged, and properly rewarded employees are loyal and productive.

Understand Your Role as CEO

Expanding generally means that your role as CEO will change over time. Managing a company with 50 employees and $5 million in sales is just not the same as managing a company with 2,000 employees and sales over $100 million. Generally, if you have decided that long-term growth is the prime objective of your company, you will likely find yourself delegating more and more of the day-to-day operations of your company to your management team, while you take more responsibility for your expansion program. This means that you have to surround yourself with highly qualified, bright, motivated, and committed people.

Not only your role as CEO will, or should, change however. As your company expands and is exposed to change and an enlarging perspective, your perspective will likely change, too. Expanding generally means that you have to face the realities of the global marketplace head-on. You will discover more competition in the form of competing products and new technologies or alternative products that put your business at risk. At the same time, you will discover new ideas that will help your business become more successful, from new ways of using supplies and suppliers to better ways of packaging and marketing, from techniques that improve the productivity of your workforce to financing possibilities that simply didn't exist in your current market. You might want to think of it as the continuing education of the CEO. The more you know and are exposed to, the better equipped you are to deal with every facet of life.

And the more you know as a CEO of a business, the more likely you are to keep your business successful. This is one of the primary challenges of expanding—how well you can put to use everything you learn during the process.

Of course your management style will be affected at the same time. Learning, absorbing everything there is to master as you expand, and putting all that knowledge to work productively means that you cannot manage in the same way you did before you began your expansion program. How you manage your company after you have got your expansion program on the road depends on the nature of your business. Generally speaking, though, your role will probably become more one of "visionary leader" than day-to-day manager. If your expansion plan is to be successful, you will have developed a management team that can keep your operations on a profitable track. You will likely become more leader than manager. You will be the one who develops, explains, and sells your five-, ten-, or twenty-year expansion plan to your management team and your entire workforce. You will be the guiding force in each phase of expansion, making the final decisions on what to pursue next, fostering the kind of commitment you need for success, and ensuring that your management team and the rest of your workforce understands at every step of the way why your company is pursuing its expansion goals. This won't leave much time for day-to-day management, but it also means there won't be too many dull moments.

Nonetheless, perhaps the greatest risk the CEO faces is getting too far away from the heart and soul of his or her business—the production of a product or providing of a service. Expanding into a new market, acquiring a competitor, selling into another country can be heady stuff. It can occupy you for months and even years on end. But you have to take time to fulfill your role as CEO—review the financial side of the business regularly, review the performance of the management team, keep an eye on production and the quality of your product and workforce, keep abreast of new technologies and products, and above all, stay in touch with your customers. They are the only reason you are in business. Of course, all this equips you better for keeping your expansion plan in high gear.

Manage the Risk Involved in Expanding

Expanding puts your company at risk. Doing nothing also puts your company at risk, probably at greater risk. As you put your expansion plan into motion, you will learn how much risk you, your management team, and your investors can tolerate. More importantly, you will learn and develop techniques to manage risk effectively, techniques that you likely would not learn if you did not commit your company to expanding. The techniques you learn, of course, can be applied to the domestic or current side of your operations.

Steering your company into change through expansion also puts you and your company's place in the industry and the business world into a more meaningful perspective. One of the most eye-opening things you probably will do while pursuing growth is visit customers around the world. During these visits, you will discover just how many dangers confront your business every day and how many opportunities exist from which your business can profit. You'll come face to face with the true meaning of risk, and you'll discover enough ideas and possibilities to keep you excited through several lifetimes.

Expanding your business successfully is about risk management, increasing profitability, and about enhancing your place in your industry. It's also about learning, about applying newfound knowledge to a business that you live and breathe, and about watching yourself, your workforce, and your company grow.

Good Luck!

APPENDIX A

Premdor's Environmental Due Diligence Checklist

Checklist for Preliminary Environmental Evaluation (Phase I Audit)

Search of Applicable Public Records with Respect to the Company's Operations

Air quality authority, fire department, ocupation health and safety authority, environmental authority, local health department, permit and license authorities, sanitation agency, water quality authority, assessment office, zoning department, underground storage tanks, any other registration and notification agencies.

Site Visit

Should include information obtained from interviews with knowledgeable parties having information about past and current activities carried on at the plant, history of the site, and potential areas of contamination.

◆ Areas of potential contamination.

◆ Areas of visible contamination.

◆ Boundaries.

◆ Description of adjacent properties and the uses conducted thereon.

◆ Description of area within 2,000 feet.

◆ Description of building materials.

◆ Description of chemical activities.

- ♦ Description of ground management practices.

- ♦ Description of site operations.

- ♦ Description of waste management practices.

- ♦ Proximity to surface water.

- ♦ Geology.

- ♦ Hydrology.

- ♦ Topography.

Interviews

- ♦ Site line personnel and manager.

- ♦ Neighbors and local parties.

- ♦ Local historians.

Areas of Concern

The report should distinguish between an insignificant and a significant or potentially significant problem that could affect the value of the business and the property.

- ♦ Adjacent properties with areas of concern.

- ♦ Asbestos-containing materials.

- ♦ Lead-containing materials.

- ♦ Enforcement activity and fines.

- ♦ Manufacturing processes that use hazardous materials.

- ♦ On-site disposal and landfill practices.

- ♦ Off-site disposal and landfill practices.

- ♦ Dust control and disposal.

- Ponds, basins, and lagoons.
- Potentially contaminated surface or groundwater.
- Spills and runoff.
- Stained and discolored soils.
- Stored hazardous materials and wastes.
- Stored hazardous wastes.
- Underground storage tanks.

Recommendations

Recommendations for further action should be based on the areas of concern. In some cases areas of concern will not involve any further investigation, while others may require a secondary investigation to obtain more precise information about potential contamination. Recommendations should be clearly stated and give clear directions.

Cost Estimates

- Cost estimates in the Preliminary Evaluation should be presented.
- Quantify the problem in terms of its potential financial impact.
- Advise as to whether further engineering work and remediation is required.

Site Plan

A simple site plan showing the site boundaries and the location of each area of concern is often useful in making a Preliminary Evaluation report a complete and easy to understand contract.

APPENDIX B

Summary of Premdor's Due Diligence Checklist

Due Diligence Checklist

Before undertaking any due diligence inquiry, consult with counsel to ensure that material and information gathered during the due diligence process will not result in the exchange of competitively sensitive information that is not necessary for evaluating the feasibility or desirability of the proposed transaction. Any material or information gathered during the due diligence process should be covered by an appropriate confidentiality agreement that limits the use of such information.

History

1. Development of major product innovations: where, when, by whom, impact on market share?

2. Major changes through the years in:

   ◆ Lines/products produced.

   ◆ Production methods.

   ◆ Marketing.

   ◆ Distribution methods.

   ◆ Management

   ◆ Plants and property.

   ◆ Financial reporting.

3. Expansion of Company (acquisitions vs. organic growth—relative contribution).

4. Susceptibility to cyclicality—changes in sales growth and margins?

   ♦ Types of cycles affecting the Company.

   ♦ Severity of impact.

5. Particular developments during the last five years.

Business and Operations

1. Breakdown of sales and profits between products/product lines sold during the last five years. If available, a similar breakdown by geographical region, distribution channel, and end-user market.

2. Complete list of products manufactured, raw materials used, and manufacturing processes.

3. Contract manufacturing agreements—if any, indicate terms, prices/formulas, termination costs.

   ♦ Method of purchase.

   ♦ Split between industrial, wholesale, and retail.

4. Percentage of revenue taken by each principal customer and industry.

5. Purchasing and suppliers.

   ♦ Purchasing policies and procedures.

   ♦ Percent under contract, open market, etc.

   ♦ How far ahead are purchases made?

   ♦ Commitments and long-term contracts—terms (amount, price, payment terms).

   ♦ General terms for purchasing.

   ♦ Special discounts received.

♦ Relationship between purchasing/inventory control.

♦ Information systems and controls used for purchasing and inventories—recent or contemplated changes?

♦ Major sources of supply/suppliers.

♦ Special or concentrated sources.

♦ Overseas sources.

♦ Recent bill samples from suppliers.

6. Inventory policies and practices.

♦ Frequency of physical inventories.

♦ Historical and current breakdown of inventory value by raw materials/WIP (work in progress)/Finished goods (by location and period). What is, if any, LIFO (last in first out) reserve?

♦ Target levels for inventory and turnover.

♦ Degree of seasonal variation in inventory levels and turnover.

♦ Systems used for inventory control—improvements or changes made and/or planned.

♦ Inventory and turnover performance over last five years compared to budget/plans. Impact of acquisitions.

♦ Current inventory status vs. "normal" levels for this time.

♦ Controls in place to limit inventory shrinkage and losses—historical and recent levels of shrinkage/losses.

♦ Matters such as pledged inventories and consigned inventories.

7. Distribution.

♦ Shipping and delivery—areas served.

♦ Transportation expenses.

- List of all distribution centers, including headcount/cost per employee at each site (if shared site, annual amount paid by company).

- Distribution mechanics—facilities and operations.

- Warehousing of inventories—where? how handled?

- Service levels.

- Fixed costs of warehouses by facility.

- Capacity and expansion plans.

- Overseas shipping, delivery, and warehousing.

- Direct sales force—headcount per regions served.

8. Sales policies and credit terms.

- Policy with respect to slow lines. Markdowns?

- Planned special or seasonal price promotions—changes in past policy.

- Seasonality of sales—trend, how managed?

- Ability to pass on increases in raw material costs and other production costs?

- Credit policies, credit terms, and methods—volume of such sales by year.

- Credit losses—trend estimates, reserves.

- Control systems used to monitor customer credit and credit losses—actual credit performance compared with planned losses.

- Return sales, damaged goods returns—history and company policy.

- Analysis of sales force—commission scheme, headcount, average compensation, average cost.

◆ Contracts with brokers and warehouses and any termination costs involved.

◆ International sales—for broker/distributors, indicate contract term and cancellation provisions.

9. Marketing.

◆ Advertising and marketing strategy—type of advertising, media used, historical changes.

◆ Advertising expenditures—historical, current, and planned.

◆ Outside sources used—advertising agencies, marketing consultants, marketing research firms?

◆ Promotion strategy and special sales programs.

◆ Success/failure of past promotional programs, method used to measure performance?

◆ Planned promotional programs.

10. Impact of changes in the value of the dollar on: sales, purchasing, production costs, taxes, other expenses, etc.

11. Research.

◆ Currently produced products developed in-house.

◆ New products under development.

◆ Number of employees in research and development.

◆ R & D expenditure.

◆ Technology licensing agreements, if any. Terms?

12. Prospects for growth in various lines/products.

13. Projections for business cycle impact on prospects for growth and margin improvement.

14. Chances of improved profitability of various lines/products.

15. Royalty arrangements (if any), brand names, trademarks, patents, and other intellectual property.

Property, Plant, and Equipment

1. Analysis of properties.

   ♦ Location.

   ♦ Form of ownership.

   ♦ Terms of leases/rentals.

   ♦ Size and capacity.

   ♦ Management.

   ♦ Condition of properties—relative to competitors.

   ♦ Depreciation policies and amortization rates.

2. Valuations of properties: appraisals, insurance valuations, assessments, revaluations—when and by whom?

3. Insurance status of properties and equipment.

4. Any existing or foreseen important developments with respect to the various properties—labor, environmental, transportation, political issues, etc.

5. Expansion possibilities of present properties.

6. Major additions/dispositions during last five years.

7. Products produced at each property.

8. Environmental litigation or exposure by property.

9. Future capital expenditure requirements.

10. Planned reorganization/restructuring of facilities.

Management

1. Officers (present and contemplated): names, ages, health, background, affiliations, responsibilities, and committee positions.

2. Changes contemplated in officers' positions and responsibilities.

3. Experience of officers.

4. Management contracts and contemplated changes.

5. Incentive plans and/or bonus plans.

   ♦ Profit sharing.

   ♦ Stock purchase.

   ♦ Pension arrangements.

6. Salary increases over last fiscal year of 10 percent or more.

7. Transactions between the company and any officer or senior management member.

   ♦ Property sales or purchases.

   ♦ Loans, borrowings, and advances.

   ♦ Other business transactions.

Employee Relations

1. Current labor force.

   ♦ Number of employees—peak, average, seasonality.

   ♦ General characteristics—age, sex, education, training, experience.

   ♦ New hiring or headcount reductions contemplated.

2. Status of relations with employees.

♦ Unions and contracts—employees covered, unusual provisions.

♦ Stability/turnover of labor force.

♦ Employment contracts and labor agreements.

♦ History of labor relations. Recent changes or foreseen problems.

♦ Competitive situation and labor supply/availability.

♦ Work hours.

3. Current training programs—recent or contemplated changes.

4. Compensation arrangements.

♦ Wage levels and contracts.

♦ Wage increases over past year and effect on annual basis beyond that shown in last year's results.

♦ Employee benefits: benefit and pension plans, insurance, post-retirement benefits, funding status.

♦ Wage increases contemplated—when, how much, estimated impact on financial results.

5. What percentage of employees work on a commission basis?

6. Details of severance plans/policies.

Accounting Review

1. Accountants/auditors for the company.

♦ History, methods, relationship, management letters.

♦ If target is in a foreign jurisdiction, difference in reporting procedures and results based on domestic and foreign GAAP (generally accepted accounting principles).

2. Working capital.

  ◆ Accounts receivable.

    ◇ Summary of accounts, including agings, by major components as of the most recent year-end and the most recent interim reporting date.

    ◇ Account write-offs, receivables with special terms (e.g., installment sales, etc.)

    ◇ Account receivables sales?

  ◆ Inventories.

    ◇ Method of valuation.

    ◇ Reserves.

  ◆ Accounts payable.

    ◇ Summary of accounts, including agings, by major components as of the most recent year-end and the most recent interim reporting date.

    ◇ Cut-off policy for monthly and year-end closings.

  ◆ Accrued liabilities.

    ◇ Summary of accrued liabilities by major components as of the most recent year-end and the most recent interim reporting date.

    ◇ Accruals for pensions, bonus/profit sharing, compensated absences, claims.

3. Accounting methods for depreciation, pension costs, revenue recognition.

Financial Review

1. Financial statements.

  ◆ Detailed P&L's (profits and losses), Balance Sheet and Cash Flow Statement (last three years) as well as pertinent notes to the financials. Information should be by country if possible.

♦ Financials excluding impact of acquisitions (if available).

♦ Internal and External audit reports, including management response letters (last two years).

♦ Is any nonvariable overhead included in Cost of Goods (e.g., utilities, mechanical labor, plant supervision and clerical, corporate allocations etc.)?

♦ Identify all allocated corporate or divisional overhead expenses included in P&L—allocation, methodology.

♦ Delinquency and loss reporting.

2. Three-year volume trend by product/lines, both domestic and international.

3. Price increases by product/product line for the last three years.

4. Summary of general and administrative expenses by natural classification.

5. Nonvariable overheads. Also, line item information by department.

6. Operating budgets for current year and succeeding year; including policies, underlying assumptions and mechanics, capex and working capital budgets.

7. Discuss liabilities not reflected in financial statements, such as: contingent liabilities, recapture tax, losses or gains on planned divestitures, deferred compensation/bonus agreements.

8. Data processing system: current equipment, software development practices and policies, current capacity, programs/applications used.

9. Amortization of goodwill and intangibles broken out from depreciation and amortization for the last three years.

Tax Review

1. Income tax returns for the preceding five years.

2. Discussion of the latest examination by relevant taxing authorities.

3. Discussion of any filings with or examinations by federal or other tax authority.

4. Where does the company currently file income and franchise tax returns, and what are the tax rates?

5. Status of any current tax examinations being conducted in non-North American jurisdictions. Any potential tax exposures in such jurisdictions?

6. Effect of proposed purchase on employee benefit plans.

7. Tax basis and fair market value of major assets, asset categories, and business segments.

Legal Review

1. History of and relationship with outside counsel.

2. Description of all relevant regulatory bodies and rules.

3. Company summaries and memoranda relating to any governmental or adminsitrative investigations, proceedings or arbitrations, whether pending, threatened or concluded, to which the company is or was subject to with respect to the business and that is material to the business; access to all relevant documentation regarding such investigations, proceedings, and arbitrations.

4. Company litigation summaries and memoranda of all outstanding litigation and all litigation settled or otherwise terminated to which the company is or was a party to with respect to the business and that are material to the business.

5. All consent decrees, court and administrative judgments and orders, settlements, etc., requiring or prohibiting future activities of the company.

6. Agreements and contracts.

- ◆ Agreements with manufacturers or others for joint advertising, merchanding, or promotion.

- ◆ Loan agreements, lines of credit, letters of credit, debt financing, capital leases, and guarantees of the business material to the business, as well as latest compliance certificates as to covenants and restrictions thereunder relating to such agreements.

- ◆ All contracts and commitments material to the business including customer agreements, supply agreements, manufacturing agreements, and other miscellaneous agreements of the company such as guarantees, agreements with competitors and government agencies, confidentiality agreements, and noncompete agreements.

- ◆ Any shareholder agreement entered into.

7. Insurance coverage.

- ◆ Schedule of insurance policies, including officer liability insurance policies.

- ◆ Summary of claims made under the Company's insurance policy in last five years.

- ◆ Correspondence with insurance companies regarding reservation of liability or rights.

- ◆ Officer indemnification agreements.

8. Documents relating to intellectual property owned or used by the Company—patents, copyrights, trademarks, service marks, licenses, and trade names.

9. Benefit plans and arrangements.

- ◆ Most recent copies of all employment, consulting and/or compensation contracts, agreements, arrangements, plans and programs (e.g., bonus, incentive, compensation, deferred compensation, capital accumulation) and qualified plans and program (e.g., pension, profit sharing) entered into, contributed to, or maintained by the Company.

Environmental Review

1. Date and result of past environmental reviews.

2. Potential environmental liabilities.

3. Reserves and anticipated outlays for environmental remediation.

Index

Acquisitions and Mergers
in 1980s, 101–2, 112, 120
assumptions about, 107
benefits of, 102–3
books on, 101
communication about, 23, 25,
    105, 123–24
and competitors, 103, 106,
    123–24
and cost of expansion, 46,
    47–48
and customers, 7, 106–8, 110–
    11, 114, 118, 124, 126
and distribution, 102, 106, 118
in the door industry, 6–8, 16, 20
and employees, 27–28, 105,
    107–9, 117–19, 122–25
failure of, 104–5, 109, 122, 125
and financing, 44, 51, 102, 105,
    107, 109–11, 113–14, 126,
    198–99
and free trade agreements, 113
and horizontal expansion, 49
and inventories, 102, 114

and management, 27, 103, 105,
    107–12, 116–18, 123–25,
    127
and marketing, 102, 106, 110
objectives of, 110, 119, 125
planning for, 105–7, 114,
    122–26
and plants, 108, 110, 114, 118,
    123
and Premdor, 7–9, 20, 24, 27,
    31, 39–40, 43, 54, 103–4,
    106, 108, 112, 116, 118–20,
    122, 125, 169
and product lines, 103, 110–11,
    116
and profitability, 15, 102, 109
by public companies, 53, 120
and rationalization, 15, 102
during recessions, 20–21, 110
and regulations, 108
risk of, 31, 121
and sensitivity analysis, 114
and shareholders, 51, 114
stages of, 107–26

Acquisitions and Merges
(*continued*)
and stock options, 28
and strategic alliances, 93
and strategies for increasing
market share, 39
during strong economic times,
21
and suppliers, 106–8, 126
and technology, 103, 110–11
timing of, 29, 104, 124
and vertical integration, 105
Advertising
See Marketing
Alliances
expansion through, 91–98, 131,
198
and exporting, 156, 175
See also Partnerships
Associations, Business
and information on exporting,
167
Assumptions
and acquisitions and mergers,
107
in business plans, 40–42, 43
and expansion into new
domestic markets, 80–81
Automobile Industry
and inventory control systems,
95
and marketing, 99
and product lines, 76–77
shifting customer preferences
in, 67, 68
and strategic alliances, 97

Bankers
and acquisitions and mergers,
107–8, 112, 114
and business plans, 38, 44
and commitment to company
growth, 30
and debt financing, 57–58
and environmental audits, 57–
58, 115
and exporting, 138, 167, 178–79
and meeting goals, 42
and mergers as a source of
financing, 51
and public companies, 53
Business Plans
See Planning

Canada
exporting to, 154, 156, 163, 164,
166
Capacity
and company growth, 17, 28–
29, 100, 193
and costs of expansion, 46, 47
and defensive strategies for
domestic markets, 66
and exporting, 138–39, 179
and plant production volumes,
37, 41
Capitalization
and expansion plans, 59
and exporting, 138, 142, 178
and franchising, 89
Century Wood Door Limited
acquisitions of, 6, 31

and merger with Premdor, 7, 8,
43, 52, 103, 118
Commerce, U.S. Department of
and information on foreign
markets, 141
Commitment
to acquisitions and mergers, 107
to company growth, 17, 18–20,
23, 32–33, 200–202, 204
to creating value for customers,
71
to exporting, 136, 148–52,
171–72
Communication
and acquisitions and mergers,
23, 25, 105, 123–24
and company growth, 17, 23–26
Computer Industry
acquisitions and mergers in, 102
Computers
and electronic data interchange
(EDI) systems, 196
and exporting, 151, 157, 184
and growth capacity, 29
and learning curves, 25
and reviewing production
processes, 195
and sensitivity analysis, 45–46
Currency
and exporting, 164–66, 185,
186–87, 200
Customers
and acquisitions and mergers, 7,
106–8, 110–11, 114, 118,
124, 126
communication with, 23, 24–26,
30

and defensive strategies for
domestic markets, 63, 66–
71, 131
and equity financing, 51
and exporting, 28, 134, 142–43,
147, 149–50, 155–63, 165–
68, 173–74, 177, 181,
183–86
feedback from, 3, 194–98
and foreign competitors, 131–
32, 144–45
and horizontal expansion, 49
loss of, 193–94
and marketing, 71–75, 100
of Premdor, 25, 69, 71, 72–76,
94–95
and public companies, 53
and purchasing power, 40–41
and regional markets, 81, 84
and selection of target markets,
85–86
strategic alliances with, 36, 91,
93–98
and strategies for increasing
market share, 39
and value-added products,
75–77
and vertical integration, 48
Cycles, Business
and acquisitions and mergers,
108, 114
and exporting, 159–60, 170, 173
and Premdor, 14, 15
reducing vulnerability to, 13,
15, 80, 82–83, 100, 193,
200

Distribution
  and acquisitions and mergers,
    102, 106, 118
  and electronic data interchange
    (EDI) systems, 196
  and expansion into new
    domestic markets, 2, 84
  and exporting, 157, 161, 174–
    75, 181–82, 185, 188
  greater taking advantage of, 13
  and regional markets, 81
  reorganization of, 7
  and strategic alliances, 93–94,
    198
  and strategies for increasing
    market share, 39, 100
Diversification
  in 1980s, 8, 14, 36, 49
  and business cycles, 100, 199,
    200
  and exporting, 134
  and Premdor, 14, 15, 22
  of product lines, 7, 14
  and reducing risk, 2
Due Diligence Process, 109,
    111–21
  Premdor's checklists for,
    209–27

Efficiency
  and acquisitions and mergers,
    102
  and company growth, 3, 7
  and exporting, 134
  and reviewing production
    processes, 195–96

Electronic Data Interchange
    (EDI) Systems, 196
Employees
  and acquisitions and mergers,
    27–28, 105, 107–9, 117–19,
    122–25
  and building a winning team, 26
  and communication about
    company growth, 23–24
  and defensive strategies for
    domestic markets, 64–65
  and exporting, 134–35, 138,
    145–52, 179–80, 188
  and fostering commitment to
    growth, 18–19, 23, 29–30,
    200–202, 204
  of Premdor, 27, 201
  and selection of target markets,
    85
  and stock options, 53
Environmental Health
  and acquisitions and mergers,
    115–16
  and debt financing, 57–58
  and Premdor's due diligence
    checklist, 209–11
European Economic Community,
    132
Exchange Rates
  See Currency
Export Development Corporation
  and information on foreign
    markets, 141
Exporting
  and adapting to foreign
    markets, 141–48

assessing potential for, 18,
    131–33
advantages of, 133–34
and business location, 22
to Canada, 154, 156, 163, 164,
    166
and capacity, 37, 138–39, 179
commitment to, 136, 148–52,
    171–72
and computers, 151, 157, 184
and corporate self-evaluations,
    137–38
and cross-border alliances, 92,
    94
and currency, 164–66, 185,
    186–87, 200
and customers, 28, 134, 142–43,
    147, 149–50, 155–63, 165–
    68, 173–74, 177, 181,
    183–86
disadvantages of, 134–35
and distribution, 157, 161, 174–
    75, 181–82, 185, 188
and employees, 134–35, 138,
    145–52, 179–80, 188
and export agents, 140, 143,
    145, 174–75, 177, 185
to Far East, 135–36, 154, 157
and financing, 142, 160–61,
    167, 178–79, 182
and free trade agreements, 135,
    154
gathering information on,
    167–70
and government assistance
    programs, 56, 141, 155,
    166, 167–69, 178–79

and inventories, 140, 178–79
and language barriers, 162–63,
    169, 177
and learning from foreign
    competitors, 143–45, 175,
    189
and management, 137–38, 143,
    148–52, 176–77, 182
and marketing, 139–40, 150,
    163–64, 174, 182
to Mexico, 135, 154, 162
and packaging requirements,
    163, 174, 182
and payment collection
    methods, 166–67, 185–86
planning for, 134, 136–37, 153,
    171–89
and plants, 134, 151, 173, 179
and political unrest, 165
of Premdor, 8–9, 133, 139–43,
    146–47, 151–52, 155–57,
    159–60, 162, 165, 168–70,
    176, 183, 186, 188–89
and prices, 139, 151, 154, 157–
    58, 160, 162, 174, 177,
    180–81, 183–88
and product lines, 134, 138–40,
    158–59, 163, 173–75,
    181–84
and profitability, 139, 151, 158,
    160, 179, 187
and regulations, 141, 147, 156,
    163–64, 168, 176–77
and relearning markets, 142
risk of, 142, 154–55, 158–59,
    170, 173, 175, 178

Exporting (*continued*)
  and sensitivity analysis, 46
  and shipping, 161, 174–75, 183,
    186, 187
  and strategic alliances, 96, 156,
    175
  during strong economic times,
    21
  and suppliers, 134, 148, 158
  and tariffs, 161, 176
  and targeting markets, 154–70
  and taxes, 141, 144, 146, 161,
    164, 176
  timing of, 177–78, 182
  and trade shows, 142, 144, 162,
    168–69
  to United States, 154, 155–56,
    166, 169
External Affairs and International
  Trade Canada, 141

Far East
  exporting to, 135–36, 154, 157
Financing
  and acquisitions and mergers,
    44, 51, 102, 105, 107, 109–
    11, 113–14, 126, 198–99
  and business plans, 43–45, 57
  and company growth, 17, 22–
    23, 198–99
  and comparisons between 1980s
    and 1990s, 36
  and competitive advantage over
    aging industries, 22
  and debt, 56–58
  and defensive strategies for
    domestic markets, 64, 66

  and equity, 50–51
  and exporting, 142, 160–61,
    167, 178–79, 182
  and franchising, 55–56, 86–87,
    91
  and interest rates, 40
  and reporting systems, 35–37,
    57
  resources for, 35–36
  and tax planning, 36–37
Food Retailers, 71–72
Foreign Competitors
  See Competitors, foreign
Foreign Markets
  See Competitors, foreign;
    Exporting
Franchising
  advantages of, 87–88
  and cost of expansion, 55–56,
    86–87
  disadvantages of, 88–91
  types of, 86–87
Free Trade Agreements
  and acquisitions and mergers,
    113
  and business changes in late
    1980s, 1
  and changing export markets,
    135, 154
  and the door industry, 6
  and globalization, 104, 132
  and partnerships between U.S.
    and Canadian companies,
    92

Globalization
  and company growth, 17

and the door industry, 6–7, 8–9, 22, 103
and increasing competition, 103–4
two-pronged strategy for, 63
Government Assistance Programs
and exporting, 141, 155, 166, 167–69, 178–79
and financing expansion, 56

Home Depot, 68
Horizontal Expansion Costs, 49

Innovation and Expansion, 75–77
Integration and Stabilizing Company Growth, 30
Inventories
and acquisitions and mergers, 102, 114
control systems for, 95
and exporting, 140, 178–79
Investment
and acquisitions and mergers, 110
and developing export markets, 187–88
and equity financing, 50–51
in privately held companies, 51
in public companies, 52, 54

Knowledge
and company growth, 17, 20–22, 202

and defensive strategies for domestic markets, 66, 77
and selecting target markets, 84–86
and strategic alliances, 94

Labor
See Employees
Language and Exporting, 162–63, 169, 177
Leveraged Buyouts
and company growth in 1980s, 4, 19
Liquidity
and investment in public companies, 52

McDonald's, 89–90
Management
and acquisitions and mergers, 27, 103, 105, 107–12, 116–18, 123–25, 127
of aging industries, 22
and company growth, 29, 203–4
and creating value for customers, 71
and cross-border alliances, 92
and debt financing, 57
and equity financing, 50–51
evaluation of, 201–2
and expansion into new domestic markets, 80
and exporting, 137–38, 143, 148–52, 176–77, 182
and franchising, 87, 90, 91

Management (*continued*)
  and narrative business plans, 42
  of Premdor, 81–82, 84
  and public companies, 54
  and regional markets, 81–82
Manufacturers
  strategic alliances with, 93
Market Share
  and acquisitions and mergers,
    105, 124
  and defensive strategies for
    domestic markets, 66, 153
  and growth climate of 1990s, 36
  and knowing customers' needs,
    69–70, 77
  and marketing, 71–75, 98
  protection of, 13
  and recessions, 21
  and strategic alliances, 98
  strategies for increasing, 39, 41
Marketing
  and acquisitions and mergers,
    102, 106, 110
  and competitive advantage over
    aging industries, 22
  and customers, 71–75, 100
  developing focus for, 82–84
  and exporting, 139–40, 150,
    163–64, 174, 182
  and franchising, 90
  and improving market share,
    71–75, 98, 100
  and Premdor, 21, 73–74, 83–84,
    98–99
  and product lines, 99
  researching new approaches to,
    196–97

and strategic alliances, 96
and trade shows, 85, 197
Markets, Domestic
  building knowledge base about,
    84–86
  and company growth, 2, 18
  defensive strategies for, 63
  and excess plant capacity, 37
  expansion into, 79–86, 131
  and mature product lines, 139
  shrinking of, 132
Markets, Foreign
  See Exporting
Markets, Regional
  and business cycles, 82–83
  and customers, 81, 84
  and franchising, 86
  and management, 81–82
  and post-World War II business
    environment, 1, 132
Mergers
  See Acquisitions and mergers
Mexico
  exporting to, 135, 154, 162
Midas Touch Syndrome, 19–20

Narrative
  of business plans, 38–43
  of exporting plans, 172–73, 179,
    181
Networking
  and gathering information on
    exporting, 167–68
Niche Players
  in export markets, 135–36, 159
  and planning for change, 33

and selection of target markets,
    83
North American Free Trade
    Agreement (NAFTA)
    See Free trade agreements

Objectives
    in acquisitions and mergers,
        110, 119, 125
    and building strategic alliances,
        93
    in business plans, 39, 43
    and developing marketing
        focus, 82–83
Organizational Charts, 32

Packaging for Exports, 163, 174,
    182
Partnerships
    and acquisitions and mergers,
        103
    and commitment to growth, 20
    and equity financing, 50
    between U.S. and Canadian
        companies, 92
    See also Alliances
People
    See Employees; Management
Planning
    and acquisitions and mergers,
        105–7, 114, 122–26
    and company self-assessment, 4,
        17
    and competitors, 40–42

and development of business
    plans, 37–46
and exporting, 134, 136–37,
    153, 171–89
and financing, 43–45, 57
and niche players, 33
and organizational charts, 32
Plants
    and acquisitions and mergers,
        108, 110, 114, 118, 123
    and capacity to produce for new
        markets, 28–29
    and excess capacity, 37
    and exporting, 134, 151, 173,
        179
    financing for, 44
    new construction of, 2
    specialization of, 7
Politics and Exporting, 165
Premdor
    acquisitions of, 7–9, 20, 24, 27,
        31, 39–40, 43, 54, 103–4,
        106, 108, 112, 116, 118–20,
        122, 125, 169
    and business cycles, 14, 15
    competitors of, 98
    and customer service, 25, 71,
        74–75, 94–95
    due diligence checklist of,
        215–27
    and economic indicators, 41
    employees of, 27, 201
    environmental due diligence
        checklist of, 209–11
    expansion strategy of, 49–50
    exporting of, 8–9, 133, 139–43,
        146–47, 151–52, 155–57,

Premdor (*continued*)
159–60, 162, 165, 168–70, 176, 183, 186, 188–89
and financing expansion ratios, 44–45
and improving profit margins, 65
manufacturing capacity of, 16
and market diversification, 14, 15, 22
and marketing, 21, 73–74, 83–84, 98–99
and meeting customers' needs, 72–74, 76
newsletter published by, 24, 125–26
and rationalization, 18, 118
and raw materials, 65
regional management of, 81–82, 84
and selling through to customers, 69
shareholders of, 52, 54
and stepped growth, 43
stock exchange listings of, 53–54
strategic alliances of, 96
and trade shows, 86, 197
and vertical integration, 48
Problems
and company growth, 14, 17, 30
and reviewing production processes, 195–96
Product Lines
and acquisitions and mergers, 103, 110–11, 116

and controlling risk, 31
and cost of expansion, 48
and customers' decision points, 70
and defensive strategies for domestic markets, 63, 66, 131
diversification of, 7, 14, 193
expansion of, 2, 15, 42, 76–77, 197–98
and exporting, 134, 138–40, 158–59, 163, 173–75, 181–84
and management structure, 202
and market share, 98
and marketing, 99
and rethinking business, 68
and reviewing production processes, 195–96
and strategic alliances, 93
and trade shows, 85
and value-added products, 75–76
Profitability
and accounting systems, 199
and acquisitions and mergers, 15, 102, 109
boosting of, 2, 13, 193
and costs of expansion, 46
and exporting, 139, 151, 158, 160, 179, 187
and financial analysis, 45
and franchising, 87–89
and strategic alliances, 97–98
Public Companies, 51–55
acquistions and mergers by, 53, 120

Rationalization
    and acquisitions and mergers,
        15, 102
    in the door industry, 18
    and Premdor, 18, 118
Raw Materials
    and company growth, 3, 29
    and defensive strategies for
        domestic markets, 64–65
    and economic outlooks, 40
    ensuring access to, 13, 193, 195
    and expansion into new
        domestic markets, 80
    exporting of, 134
    and Premdor, 65
    and vertical integration, 49
Recessions
    and acquisitions and mergers,
        20–21, 110
    and building market share, 21
    and business changes in late
        1980s, 1
    and debt financing, 57
    and the door industry, 6–7, 8
Regulations
    and acquisitions and mergers,
        108
    and economic outlooks, 40–41
    and European Economic
        Community, 132
    in foreign markets, 141, 147,
        156, 163–64, 168, 176–77
    on franchising, 88
    lessening of, 32
    and public companies, 53, 55
    and selection of target markets,
        84

Resources
    and business plans, 39
    and company growth, 16–30,
        193
    and exporting, 136, 142, 177,
        182, 185
    and financial reporting, 36
Risk
    and acquisitions and mergers,
        31, 121
    assessment of, 31–32
    and business plans, 38
    and debt financing, 56
    and environmental audits, 57–
        58, 115
    and exporting, 142, 154–55,
        158–59, 170, 173, 175, 178
    and horizontal expansion, 49
    management of, 204–5
    and merchant bankers, 58
    reduction of, 2, 50
    and technology, 203

Second Cup, Ltd., 90
Self-Assessment
    of company resources, 16–30
    and exporting, 137–43
    and planning company growth,
        4
Selling
    See Marketing
Sensitivity Analysis
    and acquisitions and mergers,
        114
    of business plans, 45–46

Sensitivity Analysis (*continued*)
  and debt financing, 57
Shareholders
  and acquisitions and mergers,
    51, 114
  and company growth, 29, 45
  of Premdor, 52, 54
  and running public companies,
    54–55
Shipping
  costs of, 161
  and exporting, 174–75, 183,
    186, 187
Stabilization and Company
  Growth, 30
Start-Up Costs, 46–47
Stock Options
  and acquisitions and mergers,
    28
  and retaining employees, 53
Strategies
  for acquisitions and mergers,
    106
  in business plans, 39
  and cost of expansion, 46
  for finding customers' decision
    points, 70
  for global expansion, 63
Suppliers
  and acquisitions and mergers,
    106–8, 126
  and complacency, 195
  and defensive strategies for
    domestic markets, 65
  and economic mindsets of
    1980s and 1990s, 92–93

  and equity financing, 51
  and exporting, 134, 148, 158
  and patience with company
    growth, 30
  and public companies, 53
  and selection of target markets,
    85
  strategic alliances with, 91,
    93–98
  and vertical integration, 49

Tariffs
  and exporting, 161, 176
  and free trade agreements, 135
  lowering of, 32
  and post-World War II business
    environment, 1, 132
Taxes
  and financial planning, 36–37
  and foreign markets, 141, 144,
    146, 161, 164, 176
  and franchising, 90
  and selection of target markets,
    85
Technology
  and acquisitions and mergers,
    103, 110–11
  and business changes in late
    1980s, 1
  and commitment to exporting,
    149–50
  and defensive strategies for
    domestic markets, 64
  and franchising, 90

and plant capacity for growth,
28
and risk, 203
Television Industry, 99
Timing
and acquisitions and mergers,
29, 104, 124
and business plans, 39, 42
of company growth, 20–21,
29–30
of exporting, 177–78, 182
and franchising, 87–88
Trade Shows
and exporting, 142, 144, 162,
168–69
and Premdor, 86, 197
and selection of target markets,
85, 197–98
Trademarks and Due Diligence
Process, 120

United States
exporting to, 154, 155–56, 166,
169

Value
and acquisitions and mergers,
109–11
creation of, 70–71
and franchising, 88–90, 91
and market share, 98
and product lines, 75–77
Venture Capitalists, 50
Vertical Integration
and acquisitions and mergers,
105
and cost of expansion, 48–49
and Premdor, 48
and strategic alliances, 94
Vulnerability Reduction, 13, 14,
15